Critical acclaim

Paul Levy has been an adaptable and constructive leader in a variety of different roles, as a regulator, as a government executive and as a hospital president. This book reflects all of that and some very good input from 12 year old girls. It is both enjoyable and informative.

John W. Rowe, former CEO, Exelon Corporation

Think this is about soccer? Think again. The sport is but an entry point to an observant, personal and trenchant analysis of managing people, situations and organizations. An essential addition to your business library.

Robert J. Ciolek,
Retired Public Sector Senior Executive

In a day and age where 'leader' is a title appropriated by tin pot despots and self-serving egotists, Paul Levy's story of servant leadership needs to be digested and considered. No industry more than health care stands in the messy intersection of public policy, academic debate, and business interest. In short, clear prose, Levy shows us how a real leader can stand in the midst of those tempestuous seas, and lead. A must read.

Jeff Swartz, Former CEO,
The Timberland Company

Until I read this book I had not appreciated what good teachers and successful CEO's have in common: that both are able to create learning environments by cultivating trust and empathy between themselves and their students and employees. These socially nurtured relationships are what inspire learning even as institutions face uncertainties because the best teachers and most innovative CEOs are bound to make mistakes, precisely because they are successful, but some do turn such mistakes into learning moments. This book is a captivating reflection of such processes written with both empathy and strategic insights regarding human behavior and organizational performance.

> **Bish Sanyal, Ford International Professor of Urban Development and Planning, Massachusetts Institute of Technology; Former Chair of the Faculty at MIT**

Paul Levy has had a remarkable career. At an exceptionally young age, he led large and critical organizations and distinguished himself, moving from one challenging setting to another, mastering new fields, assembling vigorous teams, and winning consistently. He gives us his most personal clues, the essential gifts in the softer side of management, that govern our ability to do the hardest work. It will be an enjoyable and rewarding read for the savviest and hardest bitten leader/ managers.

> **John Isaacson, President, Isaacson, Miller (Executive Search Firm)**

Paul Levy led us through Seabrook, Pilgrim and the first energy crisis as Massachusetts' top utility regulator. He salvaged the cleanup of Boston Harbor, brought order to the dean's office at Harvard Medical School, and turned around the mis-merged Beth Israel Deaconess Hospital. Now we see, through the illuminating lens of the girls' soccer team he coached, Paul's tools for leadership. They are lessons worth learning for all of us.

Larry Tye, former reporter at the *Boston Globe*, author of seven books; runs a Boston-based training program for medical journalists

Levy's metaphorical soccer book on business management provides those of us in leadership positions an opportunity to hit the reset button, while we assess our own effectiveness in today's ever changing world.

Roger Berkowitz, CEO, Legal Seafoods

Written by a highly successful practitioner who has led several major organizations, this book is filled with battlefield insights on what it takes to be an effective leader. Beguilingly, the book comfortably moves from issues in leading a sixth grade girl's soccer team to running a world-class medical facility in a seamless way. For a new CEO, this is a particularly relevant piece of work.

F. Warren McFarlan, Albert H. Gordon Professor of Business Administration, Emeritus, Harvard Business School

Paul Levy, who managed the cleanup of Boston Harbor and became the nation's most acclaimed hospital CEO, is a leader of uncommon skill and breadth. In *Goal Play!*, he offers powerful lessons in leadership by drawing on experiences ranging from coaching girls' soccer to managing the aftermath of catastrophic medical mistakes. How should a top executive communicate with front line staff, and with the outside world? How can a manager nurture great teams while celebrating superstars? How should a leader react when things go wrong ... and right? After reading this insightful, unblinkingly honest, and extremely readable book, you'll have the answers you need to be a more effective mentor, coach, and leader.

**Robert M. Wachter, MD, Professor and
Associate Chairman, Dept. of Medicine,
University of California, San Francisco**

We all are called to lead. How we work with others matters as much as what shows up on the scorecard. Levy's insights from many examples of great wins ... and painful failures on the pitch and even more so across healthcare and business provide a very practical guide for all of us. Levy draws insights from sports, healthcare, business and government to not only help teach us how to get better outcomes, but to be better guides for those we are responsible for. A ton of substance for such an enjoyable read.

**Jeff E. Thompson, CEO,
Gundersen Lutheran Health System**

"Great defenders sometimes score against themselves. Only the best defenders go out aggressively after every open ball." Leadership is indeed a balance of offense and defense, risk and responsibility. Levy's perspectives on the importance of servant leadership, building an environment of transparency, accountability and respect, and institution-wide commitment to ongoing quality improvement clearly reflect the future of health care. Perhaps the most valuable lesson he offers is that leaders at all levels are constantly growing, evolving and learning from their mistakes and their successes.

Ora Pescovitz, Executive Vice President for Medical Affairs, University of Michigan, & CEO, University of Michigan Health System

Paul Levy offers insightful lessons in leadership, cleverly weaving in delightfully up-lifting experiences from his years on the touchline to frame his powerful message. These light hearted stories, plucked from the diary of a soccer coach, offer the executive interested in any expanding their leadership skills a chalkboard full of sound "drills".

Bill Taylor, General Manager, Four Seasons Hotel Boston

Moving quickly from skimming to digesting, I found the book insightful and enjoyable. The journey, both of the leader and team, is anchored in achieving together clear aims. The story told is at times courageous, candid, exciting, and, occasionally bumpy. From the lessons learned will arise valuable opportunities for personal reflection ... for me that started with the notion of "first touch."

Jim Conway, Principal, Governance and Executive Leadership, Pascal Metrics; Former Executive Vice President and Chief Operating Officer, Dana Farber Cancer Institute

Paul Levy's book is a must read for any CEO who recognizes that the traditional hierarchical approach to leading an organization in the complexity of our times will not deliver sustained success and would like to consider another approach. Paul's book is also a great read for young leaders who want guidance as they attempt to master the challenges of leadership in times like these that are charged with volatility, complexity, uncertainty and ambiguity. Paul's advice and wisdom are served up intertwined with the metaphor of the complexities of soccer and the lessons learned by an experienced coach who has also had a remarkable career as a creative leader of large complex organizations with problems that threatened them with failure.

Eugene Lindsey, President and CEO,
Atrius Health

Levy persuasively portrays the idea of a leader as coach, as a steward of purpose who secures collaboration and commitment through a culture of trust. His insights on leadership are applicable in any work setting. The book is invaluable in furthering organizational success; not only does it address the role of the CEO but it guides the leadership development of all organizational members. This is a book replete with insight—and one of its key tenets is that truly wise leaders will recognize the wisdom of others.

David P. Boyd, Professor of Management at
Northeastern University; former Dean of the
Northeastern University Business School

Time is extremely precious—only more so when you're out trying to change the world. This book is a good use of that precious time—offering hard won insight into how we can nurture the leader in ourselves—and as importantly in those around us. Learning from what hasn't worked is as critical to that end as what has, and Paul offers inspiring—even entertaining—perspectives culled from the soccer field. It takes a certain amount of bravery to admit that we could stand to improve our own leadership styles, but as Paul's words (and actions) have shown, when it comes to leadership, bravery is the greatest gift we can give ourselves and those around us.

**Alexandra Drane, Chairman and
Chief Evangelist of Eliza Corporation**

Over the years, I have admired Paul Levy for his exceptional and courageous leadership of a $5 billion infrastructure project in the public sector, which he brought in on time and under budget, and for his turnaround of a major health institution facing bankruptcy. This book shares his insights about leadership garnered from his roles as coach of girls' soccer teams, and as an executive in the corporate board-room. It provides powerful examples of the positive impacts on performance that result from visionary leadership tactics and concepts, and will challenge corporate leaders to re-think their leadership styles.

**John Bewick, Former Massachusetts Secretary
of Environmental Affairs**

Paul Levy describes how the best leaders serve as coaches and teachers. They enable their people to make great decisions, rather than simply telling them what to do. Levy creatively blends together the lessons from two different parts of his life: the time he spent as a very successful chief executive and his many years as a youth soccer coach. If you want to be a supportive and transparent leader who gets results, you must read this book!

Michael Roberto, Trustee Professor of Management, Bryant University

The idea to make a comparative analysis between soccer coaching and management is unique, remarkable and as a sports fan, especially soccer, I must say very close to my heart. Observing the CEO's character as that of a coach is indeed unusual; however the key uniqueness that I found in the book is the empowerment of the employee at every level, the desire and willingness of the CEO to learn from any employee, in any position, and to run an organization that is completely transparent, including transparency regarding errors. This in the end is what makes the CEO not just a manager but also a leader.

Shlomo Mor-Yosef, MD, MPA, Director General, Hadassah Medical Organization, Jerusalem 2001–2011

Paul's book gives very powerful, very human, and very practical insights on how leaders can unlock amazing potential that all employees have. Anyone who reads this book will feel inspired to lead and learn.

Boris Levin, President, NP Medical Inc.

Paul Levy distills a career's worth of experience and accumulated insights into a fresh, creative take on the challenges of building a great institution. The book is a powerful exposition of the proposition that learning, both individual and collective, is the essential foundation for superior performance. Entertaining introductory vignettes about coaching girls' soccer deepen into a powerful metaphor for the idea that a leader's most powerful role is as coach. Indeed, Levy is at his most distinctive in asserting the importance of leaders knowing when to 'stay off the field' and in his reflections on what it takes to create the expectations and enabling conditions for people to take responsibility not only for their own performance, but also their own learning.

Nathaniel Foote, Partner, TruePoint

GOAL PLAY!

Leadership Lessons
from the Soccer Field

PAUL F. LEVY

Library of Congress Control Number: 2012902457

Second edition, with foreword, June 2012

ISBN-13: 978-1469978574

Dedication

In memory of
Monique Doyle Spencer,
whose "courage muscle"
brought joy, comfort,
and understanding to so many.

Foreword

In the glut of leadership books that are out there, Levy's stands out as one of the few that actually relates the lessons, what leaders must learn to do, to human scenarios that we are all familiar with—sports, coaching, adolescent girls trying to play soccer for their school or town team. By anchoring the leadership principles in the mundane affair of coaching girls soccer Levy enables us to see more clearly that what is involved is not so difficult and not so strange. In that way, we realize that the potential for leadership is within us, that all we really have to learn is when and how to apply what we already know. Rather than seeing leadership as some kind of special role that some people are given, this book brings leadership home to our daily life where it is needed just as much as it is needed in the corporate boardroom or government department. All that having been said, the main reason you should read this book is because it is fun to read.

Edgar H. Schein
Professor Emeritus
MIT Sloan School of Management
Author of *Helping: How to offer, give and receive help* (2009)

Table of Contents

Introduction

The girls who play soccer in our town's league in Eastern Massachusetts are among the luckiest kids in the world. They get to go out and play a beautiful game with their friends in a safe environment with terrific coaches and parents who support them. But there is an additional bit of magic that occurs during a game.

As the girls play, they unconsciously adapt to one another's strengths and weaknesses, creating a seamless web of teamwork. As a coach, when you see this happen, all you can do is smile. You know you had something to do with it, but you also know that something has happened among the girls themselves. It is a marvelous thing. They will remember it all their lives, but they may not entirely understand what they are remembering.

They will think their fond memories of the season had something to do with friendships or other social relationships or new skills acquired or the team's exceptional record. But there is something even more important that made the season so memorable. It is an elemental statement about the human condition: We are born to work and play together in teams. Many people do not get to experience that sense of ensemble, which requires giving enough of ourselves to let the filaments connect. That the girls discover it for themselves is very, very special. They are, indeed, the luckiest kids in the world, and we are likewise blessed in being able to share this time with them.

What does this have to do with executive leadership? Everything. Over the years, I have noticed vivid similarities between the job of the coach and the functions of executive leadership. Soccer is a metaphor for creative collaboration in a team, and coaching soccer can likewise be a metaphor for effective leadership. This book is a result of my realization that during my years of experience on the soccer field and in the C-suite I was constantly applying lessons from one venue to the other.

In over 20 years of coaching, I have worked with girls in virtually every age group, including both the highest and lowest level of players. Over the past four decades, I have run organizations ranging in size from 40 people to 7,000, and I have served as a senior level consultant to CEOs around the world. I wrote this book to share with you the key lessons from the juxtaposition of those two parts of my life—in a serious but also light-hearted way—in the hope that you might find them useful in your corporate and personal lives.

As in sports, the job of the professional leader is to enable your colleagues to learn, individually and collectively. You have a responsibility to assist their personal and professional development. Whether you are the CEO of an organization, a vice president, or a supervisor somewhere in the management structure—or even just the temporary leader of a task force—your main job is to be a coach to those working with you.

Notice that I say "with" and not "for" you. As a leader in your organization, you are the steward of the purpose of your firm or institution. After all, the organization will outlast you. Your task is to leave the company stronger than when you arrived. You must build equity, for sure, but the most important equity is the human capital of the firm. You can do this by encouraging the staff to work collaboratively and cooperatively. Your goal, indeed, is to help form an environment in which people hold themselves accountable to a standard of performance that reflects and reinforces the purpose of the company. That requires trust.

Fundamentally, an effective coach trusts and respects his players. He believes that their innate love of the game and desire to win can be harnessed to create a team that has the collective ability to succeed. My theory of management starts and ends with this premise as well: To be effective, a CEO[1] must trust his subordinates. He[2] must believe that they share values that are in consonance with the business purpose of

---

[1] For the sake of brevity, I often refer to "the job of the CEO" here and in the chapters that follow. As I just mentioned, this book is about leadership in general. Whether you are CEO or the leader of a department, division, or small working group in an organization, the same lessons apply. Indeed, try practicing this approach and these skills in your current job: Perhaps they will help you move up the corporate ladder!

[2] I use the shorthand "he" here when referring to a leader. Of course, women are in leadership positions, too, but it is awkward to keep saying "he or she." Please know that I mean no disrespect and in no way am attempting to be exclusionary.

the organization. He knows that his employees want to do well and do good and feel comfort, pride, and satisfaction in the organization as a whole and in their individual roles. He has to have faith in their individual ability to learn and grow— and he must have a similar faith that the organism as a whole can also learn and grow.

Absent this trust and faith, the CEO is left to exercise a degree of centralized control that will often fail. The corporate landscape is littered with CEOs who trusted primarily in their own judgment, whose hard-driving pursuit of their chosen corporate goal ignored market realities or commercial opportunities, or led others, consciously or not, into financial or ethical corruption.

So how do you take a diverse group of people and help them create a team that will carry out the purposes of your firm or institution? Doing so requires knowledge of how people work together, but most importantly, it requires knowledge of how people learn. Each of the chapters that follows starts with an anecdote about girls on the soccer field, and each story is a case study about the process and attributes of learning. (As usual, our children have more to teach us than we them, if we choose to pay attention.)

These stories fall into three broad categories. The first relates to understanding how your team learns. A key aspect of learning theory is that the teacher (i.e., coach or CEO) has to have sufficient empathy with the students to understand where they are in the learning process. Have they just begun to get interested in the topic? Are they at that awkward stage in which they feel distress at not yet having mastered the material? Or, have they arrived at the stage of pleasure in having incorporated a new framework into their thought patterns? Your job as coach is to be alert to these phases of learning, to apply or release pressure as the situation demands, and to be generous with positive reinforcement when your subordinates succeed.

The second category is about encouraging individuals to be creative and take chances. As in sports, risk-taking is an essential attribute of corporate and institutional success. The world is not static, and firms face unexpected external pressures from competitors, the economic environment, and technological change. Any firm, even a successful one, that relies on the status quo is sowing the seeds of its own destruction. The paradox faced by firms, though, is that the most effective change must come *from within* because it is more likely to generate staff engagement and enthusiasm, key elements of success. Change cannot come from within unless you have a culture that celebrates risk-taking and creativity.

The third category is the one that many corporate leaders will likely find the most difficult. These are stories demonstrating that a hands-off approach is generally more successful. A hearty reliance on delegation sends a clear message to your team that you trust them to want to do well and that you know that the front-line staff is often likely to come up with solutions to problems that are more effective than those delivered from the top down.

CHAPTER 1

"I just hadn't reached a conclusion."

DIFFERENT MODES OF LEARNING.

It was a crisp autumn afternoon in 2009, and I was coaching a group of 12-year-old girls. They were a terrific group, with sunny dispositions and a love of the game. But they were nowhere near the top team in their age group, because over the years they hadn't been assigned top coaches and consequently hadn't received much training in basic skills. I hoped to change that. First, though, I had to enable them to learn those skills. In doing so, I gained some key insights into the learning process that are as relevant to the work world as to the soccer field.

Let's start with some background about the game of soccer. Then, I'll tell you what happened on that particular fall day, and from there we can together explore the lessons for leading a firm or institution.

One of the most important parts of soccer is the first touch. Clearly, the object of the game is to score goals and keep your opponent from doing the same. The better you can control the ball when it comes to your feet, the easier it is to maintain possession of it and keep it moving in the right direction— eventually towards the goal. This is, however, a difficult task, which even some of the best varsity high school players have not mastered, notwithstanding a decade or more of playing. The ball bounces off their feet, sometimes by just a few inches, but that is enough for an opposing player to snatch it away or ruin an attempt to pass the ball to a teammate. Controlling the ball from the first touch is something that should be taught early in a player's career so she can practice it over and over and develop the muscle memory to implement it while under the pressure of a game situation. As a coach of young players, I view it as one of the most important parts of my job to incessantly work on this skill.

There are options for a first touch. You can trap the ball and stop the ball dead. You can pass it with a single touch to a teammate. You can touch it twice, first to control it and then to pass it along. You can dribble with it. You can shoot. But these are just the physical aspects of the skill. The most important factor for a successful first touch happens in the brain. The key is to think about what you are going to do with the ball before it gets to you. It is neurologically and technically difficult to wait until the ball has arrived and then, often under pressure from an opposing player, execute the appropriate first touch.

On that fall day, I carefully explained all of this to the girls. I emphasized the need to think ahead. I clearly explained that if they waited until the ball arrived, they would be under too much pressure to do the right thing.

Then I started a passing drill, and 30 seconds later a ball arrived at Margaret's feet. Despite my elaborate lesson, she reflexively booted it away to nowhere.

Our conversation afterwards went something like this:

Me: "Margaret, you weren't thinking about the ball before it got to you!"

Margaret: "Yes, Coach, I was thinking about it. I just hadn't reached a conclusion."

This simple comment was a sharp reminder that people learn in different ways and at their own pace. If your job is to be sufficiently empathic to help them through the learning process, you must be cognizant and respectful of different learning styles and speeds, and you must adjust your training approach accordingly.

In the corporate world, the equivalent of the first touch is the interactions your staff people have with others. If adult Margaret (now in the corporate setting) knows that she will be meeting with someone to plan a new project, discuss a policy, or resolve a dispute, she will find that it is much better to plan what she is trying to accomplish and how she will do so long before she sits around the table. Thinking strategically and tactically about your options, and about your interests and the interests of the other parties, allows you to formulate approaches to the issues and the processes that are much more likely to be successful.

This is one of many types of skills you as leader can pass on to your colleagues. This particular one is based on principles of negotiation, an area in which a great deal of empirical research offers guidance.[3] Of course this is just one example. You may want to work on other skills such as financial analysis, writing, oral presentations, root cause analyses, and the like.

The challenge we face, which Margaret highlighted for me, is that just telling someone something doesn't always work. We can explain all of the reasons and logic behind what we are trying to get her to do, and it still may not sink in. Where does this leave you as a leader? You need to find a way to engage your subordinates in the learning process. But there is something even more exciting and challenging at play in an organization. There, your job is not only to enable a single person to learn but also to enable groups—indeed, the whole organization—to learn.

Whatever the skill sets you are trying to impart—whether to an individual or a group—how do you do so in a consistently effective way given the different learning styles that our soccer

---

[3] Lax, David A., and James K. Sebenius. *The Manager as Negotiator: Bargaining for Cooperation and Competitive Gain.* N.Y.: Free Press, 1986.

player Margaret brings to mind? I have found that Socrates had the answer: Educate through inquiry.

Enable Adaptive Learning

Building on Socrates' theories, Ronald A. Heifetz, known for his seminal work in learning and leadership, notes:

> Unlike rote learning situations in which the answer is supplied ... by the teacher, adaptive learning situations demand that people discover, invent, and take responsibility. Leadership is a special sort of educating in which the teacher raises problems, questions, options, interpretations, and per-spectives, often without answers, gauging all the while when to push through and when to hold steady.[4]

Under this model, your trainees set the pace of learning. This was not how I had tried to teach the girls. Instead, I had engaged in a didactic approach: "Do this!" Imagine if, instead, I had spent some time asking them the questions that would have led to the desired result. "What are you thinking about as the ball is rolling to you?" "What do you want to think about?" "What game/exercise could we invent to practice that?" "How can we keep track of how well we do it?"

It might seem like it would take longer to teach in this manner, but it is actually more efficient. The time spent up front in inquiry and self-training turns out to be far less than

---

[4] Heifetz, Ronald A. *Leadership Without Easy Answers*. Belknap Press, Cambridge, MA. 1994. pp 244–245.

the time wasted by the miscues and errors and forgetfulness associated with rote learning.

In my corporate life, I came to this realization inadvertently. It was 1999, and I had already had several leadership positions and taught many classes as a faculty member at MIT. Now, though, I was Executive Dean for Administration at Harvard Medical School, and I thought it would be fun to watch how some of our brilliant faculty shoved medical knowledge into the heads of some of our equally brilliant students.

HMS uses a tutorial approach to teach much of the curriculum. I attended a session on chronic obstructive pulmonary disease (COPD). There were ten or twelve students being "taught" by a professor, but he didn't say much. I learned that in the previous session, he had posed a question and a student had been assigned to lead the next class discussion. In the class I attended, the student began, and a back-and-forth emerged with the other students. From time to time, but not often, the professor would say, "Why do you think that?" or, "What would be the implications of that conclusion?" or some such open-ended question. I could see the students work through the problem—individually and as a team—learning the lesson of the day. I could see the professor's display of empathy as they struggled to apply facts and judgment to a new set of problems and the positive reinforcement he demonstrated as they finally found pleasure in their accomplishments. He then set forth a related assignment for the next class: He showed them two charts related to lung function and said, "At our next class, please be prepared to explain the relationship between these two charts." Note the open-ended nature of the assignment. It was not, "Please present a list of the symptoms of COPD." To fulfill the assignment, they would not just need to know the symptoms. They would also have to incorporate them within a broader understanding of the respiratory system.

In later months and years, I extrapolated from this experience and applied it in my leadership roles. I reasoned that if I wanted to create an environment that would enable people to learn in the context of solving corporate problems, I would need to create a structure that supported a more effective approach to learning. So, turning back to Socrates and Heifitz, I started to apply this approach in meetings in my office and conference rooms. I would pose the opening question but not offer an opinion or bias to the others. I would ask what I tended to call "dumb questions:" What data do we have to support that conclusion? Are we asking the right questions? Should we be bringing in other people or resources to get the right answer?

The meetings would progress in a very democratic fashion. Everyone's point of view was valued, regardless of his or her place in the organization. Participants felt engaged and even excited by the interaction and vibrancy of the discussion. My comments displayed empathy, support, and encouragement for the learning process. We were all learning together.

All? Yes, especially me. I had the advantage of watching a group of committed, experienced, dedicated people play out options, ideas, and concerns right in front of me. Since I was not invested in a particular answer, I could keep an open mind and gain insights about the topic at hand, while also thinking about the implications for broader strategic issues. The less I said and did, the smarter I got.

I can already sense some readers getting edgy. Some might be feeling that they would be seen as weak or indecisive if they behaved in this manner. Others might fear that the group would come to a different conclusion than their own. "What if I know the right answer or have a strong feeling about how we should proceed? Don't I have an obligation to push the group in that direction?"

It is certainly fine to have your own ideas about how to resolve a thorny business issue. And, in certain settings, it is all right to impose them on the group. There is an apocryphal story about President Abraham Lincoln at a cabinet meeting. He asked the group to discuss whether to take the controversial step of issuing an Emancipation Proclamation. They unanimously recommended against it. His response, "Seven nays, and one aye; the ayes have it." He knew that his proposal was too politically explosive to be approved by a consensus-driven cabinet.

Sometimes, too, you find yourself leading a particularly stubborn organization, one to which the kind of open participation we have been discussing is a foreign concept. You might be facing a serious and important problem. Then, you need to be firm and more direct in leading people to the kind of solution you have in mind. Here's an example from the Massachusetts state government.

Cowbells Solve the Problem:
Some Groups Need Extra Direction

When Bill Geary took over as Commissioner of the Metropolitan District Commission (the regional parks and roadway agency for the Boston area) in 1983, he noticed an odd traffic phenomenon. About once a week, a truck that was too tall would enter one of the two main roads along the Charles River—Storrow Drive or Memorial Drive and attempt to go through the underpasses below the main bridge crossing at Massachusetts Avenue. Those underpasses had only nine feet of headroom. The truck would hit the bottom of the bridge assembly, its roof would roll up like the top of a sardine can, and it would get stuck, blocking one or both of the two lanes of traffic. Traffic would back up two miles or more. The MDC police and road crews would go to work, rescue the truck driver, deflate the tires, and tow the truck away. Meanwhile, thousands of drivers would be delayed.

On the Cambridge side, the freshmen women living in MIT's McCormick Hall would at first jump with a start when they heard a crash and would watch the rescue operation. By second semester, they had become so accustomed to this pattern that they didn't even look up from their homework.

Bill brought his team together and suggested that having a truck crash into a bridge every week was not acceptable. Couldn't something be done? "No, Commissioner," he was told. "Besides, we have a routine all worked out. The police handle the traffic. We bring in the tow truck, the Jaws of Life to pry open the crushed vehicle, whatever we need. We clean out the whole problem within an hour."

Bill had been around state government long enough to understand the institutional environment he faced. For years, the MDC was the resting place of hundreds of patronage appointments. Many people in the agency owed their jobs to a legislative "sponsor," a member of the state Senate or House of Representatives who had prevailed upon a previous commissioner to hire a friend, a relative, or a friend or relative of a friend or relative. Most of the world is characterized by six degrees of separation. At the MDC, it was two degrees. Employees had a lifetime sinecure that allowed them to retire with a pension worth 80 percent of their highest salary, not to mention health care and other benefits.

Bill liked to describe the MDC as an agency where "the momentum is with inertia." In other words, people could always find an excuse not to do something. Indeed, they had been trained to be that way over the decades. It was *never* to your advantage, as a staff member, to make a creative suggestion or take initiative. If your suggestion went awry, you would be blamed. If it worked, you would never get credit; you would more likely be ostracized by your fellow workers. After all, if your idea resulted in greater efficiency, it might suggest that someone's job was not necessary. Or if another improvement resulted, it was, effectively, a reproach of one or more of your colleagues, who had been doing it the old way for decades.

Bill knew that, in this inertia-laden environment, he was going to have to lead his staff to a solution to the truck crashes.

"What if," he said, "we put signs up at every entrance to the river roads, at the height of the underpasses, with a pictogram warning taller trucks to stay out?"

"Commissioner," someone replied, "Can you imagine the liability if our sign breaks a windshield and sends glass flying into the face of a truck driver?"

"Well, what if we make the signs out of rubber so they don't break the windows?"

"Rubber signs, Commissioner? There is no such thing."

This stymied Bill for a while. He didn't have the facts at hand to rebut this assertion. Luckily, shortly after this conversation, Bill was driving his car along the Massachusetts Turnpike when he approached a toll booth displaying an elevated sign saying, "Cars only." He looked closely. The sign appeared to be made of rubber. He stopped in the toll plaza, climbed up onto the hood of his car, and grabbed the sign. It was made of rubber!

He got on the phone and called Jack Driscoll, then head of the Turnpike Authority, and found out where he had purchased the signs.

At the next meeting with his staff, Bill reported that he had found rubber signs and suggested that they be ordered.

"But Commissioner," someone said, "What good is a rubber sign? Truck cabs are noisy places. A trucker will just hit the sign and drive right through without even hearing that he has hit it."

"Well, then, let's hang cow bells on each sign, so drivers will hear a noise as they approach our roadway if their vehicle is too high to go through the underpass."

"Where will we get cow bells?" he was asked.

"I don't know. Call a dairy farmer and ask where they get their cowbells."

The signs were installed, cow bells and all:

The frequency of crashes in the underpasses went from one per week to less than one per year. Absent Bill's persistence and personal involvement, we would still be cleaning up those weekly truck crashes three decades later.

Enraged! Some People Need Extra Attention

As you seek to get to the point where you can rely on your group's decision-making processes, and as you engage in leadership that empowers your staff, you may find that other surprises arise, deriving from entrenched behavioral patterns. Here's an example.

As soon as Amy Schectman was hired as CEO of Jewish Community Housing for the Elderly, a not-for-profit group in the Boston area, she began a process of leadership development for her top-level managers. They were well-intentioned and experienced people with a wide range of responsibilities who ran the various housing developments. The housing units had apartments, of course, but there was also a food service to operate, as well as many service programs for the seniors. But as well-intentioned and experienced as they were, these managers had not had much chance to develop leadership skills of the sort we have just discussed. As a result, meetings among the senior team were often inefficient and inconclusive. People would come in and propound strongly stated opinions. Sometimes they were based on experience. Sometimes they were based on belief. Sometimes they were based on fear of change. The opinions of the senior team often conflicted. Positions would harden, and paralysis would result. Or sometimes, the meetings had an entirely different character. In these, a particularly domineering manager would take charge, run roughshod over others, and drive the decision in a particular direction.

About a year after Amy's arrival, one manager came to her and said that there was an unresolved issue in her building. The roof was in disrepair and needed fixing, but there were many variables to consider. When should it be done? What physical process of repair would be best? How would they deal with disruption to tenants? Marcia was afraid that if she brought together all of the other managers whose jurisdictions might overlap on this problem, each would have a position on how it should be handled. How would they ever reach consensus and make a timely decision?

With some coaching from Amy, Marcia came into the meeting with a strategy. She did lots of research, organized the relevant materials, and set forth the problem. Then, rather than setting forth her view, she asked for advice. When people made statements, she quietly and persistently asked the "dumb questions." "Oh, why do you think that is a good way to proceed?" "What do others think about that?" "How will our tenants react if we do it that way?" Her questions were respectful of everyone's prerogatives, experience, and good intentions. The questions led to a rigorous and well-reasoned discussion of the options. A consensus emerged. After an hour, all agreed on the plan of action, and it could go forward.

A couple of days after the meeting, Amy ran into Marcia and tried to apply some doses of positive reinforcement. In Amy's view, Marcia deserved plenty of credit. Like Margaret eventually learned on the soccer field, Marcia had thought through her "first touch" by preparing her strategy and approach to the meeting. But something even better had happened. She had learned how to be hard on the problem but gentle on the participants. She had learned to be the coach!

But Amy found that her offer of praise was met by a sour disposition and fiery glances. "Is there something the matter?" she inquired. Marcia responded:

"I am ENRAGED! I did all this research and had a clear sense of what we should do to fix the roof and how we should do it. But you made me ask other people's opinions. It was MY TURN to decide this, and you took that opportunity away from me!"

This was not at all the reaction Amy expected. Despite her understandable surprise, she was able to hold herself together and calmly respond. She recognized the need to more deeply explain why she had encouraged Marcia to be more inclusive with her colleagues. She explained that under her administration, the kind of meeting that Marcia had so ably run was exactly what she was hoping for. Respect, consultation, and collaboration would be the watchwords. There would not be meetings where one person got to dominate the discussion and have his or her way. "Don't you think that will be more pleasant and effective?" she asked. This seemed to resonate with Marcia. She allowed as to how she would find that more comfortable and engaging. She walked off with a smile on her face and a sense of accomplishment.

I am not going to suggest to you that the challenging attitudes expressed in these examples are rare. You should be alert to the possibility that the kinds of leadership action presented here may be necessary, especially in the early days before you have been able to exert a deep influence on your organization's culture. But, even then, this sort of intervention by the leader should be reserved for those cases in which a strong stand is needed to implement a tough and potentially unpopular choice, like Lincoln's; or where the organization is so calcified that the leader has to constantly prod people to keep anything moving, like Bill Geary's MDC; or where a dysfunctional culture is so embedded that personal counseling might be necessary, as Amy Schectman found.

With time and persistent attention by the leader to the dynamics of his or her organization, the dividends will become evident. You will be able to get over your feeling of edginess in letting the team define the solution. For most issues and in most organizations, a recommendation presented by a group that has been engaged in a rigorous and thoughtful discussion is likely to be more on target than the intuitive musings of the CEO. Also, as we will discuss in future chapters, such recommendations are more likely to have the support of the various constituencies in your organization, facilitating their implementation. First, though, let's turn to the issue of how a leader can create a learning environment.

Creating a Learning Environment: Value Everybody

In order to best take into account the various learning styles of your staff members, you need to create a setting that permits them to be effectively employed. It almost seems too simplistic to say, but a person cannot engage in his or her approach to learning if the overall environment is not open and conducive to the kind of mental experimentation and exploration in which he or she needs to engage. That it takes time to learn is evident. That a person needs to be made to feel comfortable taking that time should be equally so. This sense of comfort comes when an organization clearly values one's activity, but people only feel that their activity is valued if they are *personally* valued.

Accordingly, if you as a leader are interested in creating successful learning, you need to make clear what I have mentioned above: *Everyone's point of view is valued, regardless of his or her place in the organization.* As Alcoa's former CEO Paul O'Neill put it, each person should be able to say that "I am treated with dignity and respect by everyone I encounter, every day. (Without regard to my ethnicity, my title, my pay grade or rank, the duties I perform, my educational attainment, or any other distinguishing characteristic.)"[5] In the coming chapters, you will see that I put a huge emphasis on the power of process improvement that can come from the front-line staff. A leader tends to trust and value his or her senior management team, and this is essential. In order to be truly effective, however, you need to also trust everyone in the organization and understand the value they bring to solving problems and creating strategically important initiatives. We must go overboard in making it comfortable for "lower level" staff people to present their points of view. Let me give an example:

---

[5] O'Neill, Paul, "The Key Leadership Behaviors in a Lean Organization?" ThedaCare Center for Healthcare Value, http://networkedblogs.com/ol8i9

John Rowe was CEO of New England Electric System, a large regional utility company. In the 1990s, the electric power industry was facing immense challenges. There had been cost overruns associated with huge nuclear power plants. As a result of federal legislation designed to diversify the nation's power sources, the utilities had also been required to sign uneconomic power supply contracts with small-scale hydro-electric plants, cogeneration units, and other "qualified facilities." Retail rates soared while, paradoxically, there were massive reserves of lower priced wholesale power available. Large commercial and industrial users were seeking discounts, arguing that they should get direct access to those lower wholesale prices. Absent that, they argued, they would move their companies to other parts of the United States, where electricity rates were lower. If either of those events occurred, the remaining sunk costs would be spread over a smaller base of retail customers, creating a vicious cycle of rate increases, customer departures, and further rate increases.

This phenomenon was threatening to bankrupt the electric utilities. After all, they couldn't thrive, or even survive, in a world of ever higher prices and ever fewer customers. Eventually, they would be hit with a huge bolus of "stranded costs," power supply costs that would exceed the equity in the firms. In other words, the stakes were very high.

As a leader in the field, John understood that a massive restructuring of the entire industry and the relationship with its regulators was necessary. This would take legislation in all of the states in which the company operated, settings in which there were powerful political and economic interests from multiple directions. A brilliant lawyer and finance and public policy expert, John clearly had his own ideas as to how this restructuring should take place, but he never set forth that scenario. Instead, he worked with his leadership team to define the nature of the problem, and then he left it to them to come up with options and approaches for dealing with it. He also brought in the best and brightest industry consultants to advise the firm.

At one of the most important meetings on the topic, one that would lead to codifying the company's proposal to the state legislatures and other governmental authorities, the room was packed with the country's foremost experts and all of the senior management. John set the stage with some opening remarks. The first comment came from the back of the room, not from one of the high level executives, but from a third level financial analyst in the company. It was something like, "John, I think you have misconstrued this point, and we need to make sure we get that straight before we reach our policy recommendations." This is the sort of comment that could get a junior staffer in trouble. Some might even consider it insubordination. But not here.

This CEO's response was immediate and direct: "Thank you so much for bringing that up. You are right. I got it wrong. That was an important point. Thank you." I was struck by two things. First, John's reaction was impressive and, I dare say unusual, for a CEO. I then thought how brave the young man had been to speak. I quickly realized, though, this wasn't quite true. If he had been brave, there would have been twittering in the room or knowing glances among the senior executives in the nature of, "Wait till he gets back to the office. He'll get an earful from his supervisor for contradicting the CEO." But no. John had long ago established an environment in the company in which everyone was expected to participate, where all were welcome to offer their thoughts.

The young man, then, hadn't been acting bravely. He was just doing his job. John, the leader, had made sure that such participation was valued, expected, and encouraged. In this specific case, the plan adopted by the company was stronger for the participation of this young man. His story also exemplifies the larger lesson: Individual and group learning will not occur in an organization if this ethic of encouraging individual participation is missing from the corporate culture. Why do I call it an "ethic"? Because it is fundamentally based on respect for the individual, regardless of his or her position in the firm. Only the leader can make sure that this ethic is present and dominant in the company. As we will discuss below, CEO should stand for "chief ethics officer," the person who models, insists on, and celebrates an environment of respect, trust, and appreciation for all people in the organization. He knows that a deficit on this front will kill a learning environment. Absent a learning environment, any firm is on the downward slope to obsolescence and irrelevance.

Don't Just Feel Empathy: Show It

Before we move on to the next chapter, let me leave you with one more thought. Earlier, I talked about the need for empathy in the learning process, to help people through the three stages of learning: interest, discomfort, and pleasure. But, as a leader, it is not enough to be empathetic during the learning process. It is also essential to *demonstrate* empathy, to show that you understand what employees are going through as they work through problems.

I learned how not to do this while running the Massachusetts Water Resources Authority in the 1980s. This agency was responsible for providing water and sewerage service to the Boston metropolitan area, with a staff of about 1,600, an operating budget of over $200 million, and a $3 billion capital budget. As is often the case in the corporate world, when the organization was facing an important budgetary or policy issue, the staff involved would write a comprehensive memo outlining the nature of the problem and the options before us, and recommend a solution. Our staff at the MWRA was very competent, and the memos I received were generally complete and analytically rigorous.

So, the time would come for my meeting with the authors of the memo. To be respectful, I would have read the document beforehand. They would come into the meeting and I would immediately say, "Thanks for your memo. It is an excellent summary. I agree with your recommendation. Let's proceed. Do we have anything more to discuss?" Stunned, they would sit there with nothing to add, and they would file out of my office … but not before I took their memo and threw it in the trash. After all, I figured, they had a copy and the issue had been decided. Why did I need it cluttering up my desk?

Of course, in so doing, I was not being respectful of their need to spend some time recapitulating their thinking and learning process. They may have been concerned that I had not really understood all the ramifications of their analysis or recommendation. Additionally, I should have acknowledged the work they had done—the interest, distress, and pleasure they had experienced in tackling a tough issue. Imagine how they must have felt as their document headed towards the trash bin!

Fortunately, one of my close assistants attended one of these meetings and pointed out my mistake. From then on, I took the time to explore with my staff how they had reached their conclusions.

A few years later, my training came in handy. We suffered a construction disaster while drilling a tunnel for a sewer line in one of Boston's suburbs. The tunnel boring machine became trapped behind a huge boulder 18 meters below the surface. The "mole" could not move backward either, because the sewer pipe had gotten jacked in behind it, narrowing the diameter of the escape route. It was a public relations embarrassment and a costly problem.

There were numerous theories as to how to resolve the issue.[6] As CEO, I made an obligatory visit to the town and met with the construction manager, the engineers, and the contractor. Even though I knew the whole story, I encouraged them to present it, compare the options, and recommend a solution. I respectfully asked a number of questions, even though I was

---

[6] "Sewer Infrastructure, An Orphan of Our Times," *Oceanus*. Volume 36, No 1. Spring 1993.

fairly certain they had already come up with the best solution. Then I said, "Thank you for such a comprehensive briefing. It seems to me that you have all thought this through very clearly. I agree with your recommendation. Please proceed."

I heard later from my staff that I had left a very positive impression with the engineers and contractors in that they felt I fully understood what they had gone through and their decision-making process. As a result, they felt even more confident in proceeding with their proposed plan. My empathy had paid off.

CHAPTER 2

"I am a great defender!"

LEARNING FROM MISTAKES.

I recently had lunch with one of my soccer alumnae, now aged 28. Tovah said to me, "Do you remember that play I made in the tournament we went to in Connecticut?"

Tovah (back row, fourth from left) and mates at age 14

Even though 14 years had passed, I remembered her gutsy play with clarity: "Of course, you made a great save in front of the goal." Our team's goalie had run out to clear a ball, but an opponent had taken possession and fired point-blank at our net. Tovah had hustled over to stand in front of the goal and used her chest to block the shot.

"I don't remember that," she said, "I mean when I mistakenly headed the ball into our own goal and caused us to lose the game."

"I forget that one," I replied.

"Well, I was devastated and was sitting on the grass after the game, sobbing my heart out. You came over and said, 'Don't worry, Tovah, great defenders sometimes score against themselves. Only the best defenders go out aggressively after every open ball. Every now and then, it deflects and goes into the net. You did a wonderful job.' I stopped crying, stood up, brushed myself off, and walked away smiling, saying to myself, 'I'm a great defender!' That season was very meaningful to me."

She remembered this 14 years later.

You never know when a kind or supportive word from you will make a lasting difference. Whether you intend to be or not, you are a role model and your opinion counts. When you offer solace or encouragement to someone who has made a mistake, it can make a difference. To do so, though, you must truly believe that it is not the mistake that matters, but the lesson that can be drawn from it.

But let's take this idea even further: As a leader, you must do everything you can to encourage people to admit mistakes they have made and to call out problems they have found in the organization. If people think they will get in trouble for having erred, or for having brought up a systemic problem in the organization, those errors and problems will go unreported. The person *and* the organization will thereby lose an opportunity to grow and improve. Accordingly, a strong commitment not only to transparency but to a just culture is essential to achieve continuous improvement.

Putting This in Practice: The "Never" Event

You can see this philosophy in action through an event that happened at Beth Israel Deaconess Medical Center in July of 2008. A patient woke up after orthopaedic surgery and asked her doctor, "Why is the bandage on my right ankle instead of my left ankle?" It was at that moment that the surgeon realized he had operated on the wrong limb. It is impossible to know who was more distraught, the patient or the doctor who realized that he had violated a life-long oath to "do no harm."

The surgeon immediately notified his chief of service and me, the CEO. After all of our department chiefs and quality assurance staff met to review the underlying causes of the error, we unanimously decided to publicize the case broadly throughout the hospital. We did so out of the belief that there were lessons to be learned about pre-operative procedures, which would affect the hundreds of doctors, nurses, surgery technicians, and residents engaged in surgeries at our hospital.

I also published the story on my blog in the hope that our experience might be of value to workers in other hospitals.

It was quite clear that the hospital's "time-out" protocol, which was designed to avoid precisely this kind of error, had not been properly carried out. In the weeks following this disclosure, a number of people asked me if we intended to punish the surgeon in charge of the case, as well as others in the OR who had not adhered to that procedure. Some were surprised by my answer, which was, "No."

I felt that those involved had been punished enough by the searing experience of the event. They were devastated by their error and by the realization that they had participated in an event that unnecessarily hurt a patient. Further, the surgeon immediately reported the error to his chief and to me and took all appropriate actions to disclose and apologize to the patient. He also participated openly and honestly in the case review.

My reaction was supported by one of our trustees, who likewise responded, "God has already taken care of the punishment." He pointed out that it would be hard to imagine a punishment greater than the self-imposed distress that the surgeon already felt. He had taken a professional oath to do no harm, and here he had, in fact, done harm. But another trustee said that it just didn't feel right that this highly trained physician, "who should have known better," would not be punished. "Wouldn't someone in another field be disciplined for an equivalent error?" he asked.

This was a healthy debate for us to have, but a wise comment by a colleague made me realize that I was over-emphasizing the wrong point (i.e., the doctor's sense of regret) and not clearly enunciating the full reason for my conclusion. The head of our faculty practice put it better than I had, "If our goal is to reduce the likelihood of this kind of error in the future, the probability of achieving that is much greater if these staff members are not punished than if they are."

I think he was exactly right, and I believe this is the heart of the logic shared by our chiefs of service during their review of the case. Punishment in this situation was more likely to contribute to a culture of hiding errors rather than admitting them. And it was only by nurturing a culture in which people freely disclose errors that the hospital as a whole could focus on the human and systemic determinants of those errors.

Forgiveness Coupons

Sometimes, leaders can use small symbolic acts to help reinforce the idea that mistakes are welcome and should be shared. President Bill Clinton appointed Daniel Beard to be commissioner of the Bureau of Reclamation, arguably one of the most calcified federal agencies. The BoR had built many of the nation's dams and had become focused on the mission of maintaining and building still more of them. Daniel realized that public support for large public works had waned. He reasoned, though, that an agency that owned and operated dams and watersheds had the potential to be a tremendous advocate for environmental protection, but he needed to change the mindset of his bureaucrats to embrace that broader mission.

Like Bill Geary's MDC described in Chapter 1, managers at the BoR learned early on not to take chances or be creative. "Keep your head down, and just do your job," was the watchword. But Dan had a great vision for this agency and wanted to stimulate new ideas. He especially wanted to empower managers in the 35 far-flung regional offices across the country. As part of shifting authority from the central administration to the regional directors, he issued "forgiveness coupons" to his managers and said, "Whenever you make a mistake, just hand one of these in." The coupons said on them, "It is easier to get forgiveness than permission."

To get things started, Dan personally handed two to each manager, saying they could get additional ones as they used them up. One manager said, "What if we don't use them up?" Dan replied, "Then you are in the wrong agency."

Roger Patterson, a regional director, was one senior manager who took this to heart. Patterson wanted to change the approval process for building fish ladders around dams. These allow fish to swim upstream and spawn. Previously, the approval process for this kind of construction would involve 21 steps and take three years. Patterson changed the process in the Sacramento office so that it only took eight steps and could be completed in six months. "Once, approval took a fish's lifetime. Now, it's a single spawning season."[7]

Don't You Ever Punish?

We are left, though, with a follow-on question: Under which circumstances does the need to punish someone for a mistake trump the other concerns about institutional learning and a no-blame environment? Beyond the obvious case in which a doctor or nurse intentionally harms a patient—where no one would doubt the application of punishment—I am afraid that the answer is: It depends.

A couple of years before this wrong-site case, a doctor intentionally left the operating room to consult on another patient in another building while his first patient was in mid-surgery. His logic was that there was a natural break in the procedure during which a tourniquet had to be released for a period of time to allow blood flow to return to the limb. The doctor felt that there was no risk to the patient by his absence. However, he left no attending physician in the room, only residents—a clear violation of the rules. No harm whatsoever befell the patient, who in fact was ultimately very grateful to this surgeon for completing a very complicated procedure.

Upon review of this case, our Medical Executive Committee felt that the violation of an important rule was so clear that

---

[7] "Creating government that works better and costs less," Report of the National Performance Review, Vice-President Albert Gore, Jr. Diane Publishing, July 1, 1994. p. 14.

the surgeon should be penalized, and he was suspended for a period of time and the case was reported to the state licensing board.

What distinguishes a case like that from one in which our surgeon failed to conduct a time-out before beginning the operation? Partly, it was the fact that there had recently been a widely publicized case at another hospital in town, where a surgeon left the OR and put a patient more at risk. Because of that, sensitivity to this category of events was raised. But also, our MEC response had a lot to do with its conclusion that the surgeon had *knowingly* and *intentionally* left the room unsupervised, feeling that the rule didn't really apply to him.

Is that distinguishable from failing to conduct a time-out before a surgical case? Intent should matter. In the wrong-side case, the surgeon clearly did not intend to skip the time-out. His mind was on other things, and he did it inadvertently. While that is, in great measure, his fault, it also suggested to us hospital leaders that there was a flaw either in the training *we* provided or in the procedures *we* implemented. Among other things, no one else in the room thought to mention the lapse to the surgeon as the procedure began. In other words, we participated in this error by not having the wisdom to design a sufficiently fail-safe system that would protect the surgeon (and, of course, the patient) from inadvertently missing the time-out.

Why would I suggest that we, as leaders, participated in the error if we were not present at the time of the surgery? This gets to the nature of errors in a complex environment. I'll use the time-out protocol as an example. At one level, a time-out is pretty simple: Before surgery starts, the surgeon is supposed to make sure everyone in the operating room pauses and thinks about the forthcoming case. Do we have the right patient? Check. Do we all know which procedure is about to occur? Check. Do we have all the necessary equipment and supplies? Check. Do we all agree which limb (left or right) is to be cut open? Check. Is that limb marked? Check.

On the one hand, this a simple check list, right? Just like that used by airline pilots. But notwithstanding the existence of this protocol throughout the world, hundreds of wrong site surgeries take place every year. Indeed, there has been virtually no change in the rate of wrong site surgeries in the United States over the past several years, even though they are considered "never" events, where neither the hospital nor the doctor can be paid for the procedure. While it is tempting to blame these mistakes on the surgeons, the problem is more often systemic, lying in the design of the work environment and in the performance of the team. As we shall see below, it is the job of the leader to deal with those systemic problems. One part of doing so is to ensure that the team is properly trained. Let's look at how well this works when it is accomplished, and the consequences when it is not.

Lessons from Crew Resource Management

Most people know of airline Captain Chesley "Sully" Sullenberger from the dramatic Hudson River emergency landing in

January of 2009,[8] but few are aware that he also is an expert on quality and safety improvement in the air transport industry. He has in fact discussed possible applications of lessons learned from that industry to the health care field. Referring to the use of checklists, he has said, "A checklist alone is not sufficient. What makes it effective are the attitude, behavior and teamwork that go along with the use of it."

This idea is embodied in a philosophy and set of techniques and learned behavior called crew resource management (CRM) that Sully often talks about. He explains that, in the hierarchical environment of an OR, the surgeon (like a pilot) is afforded tremendous respect and deference by the assembled team. When he is about to make a mistake, it is very hard for a subordinate to point out the pending error. However, with the tools of CRM, everybody is empowered and encouraged to speak up to anyone about what might be going wrong. Sully defines CRM as "a compact, with defined goals and responsibilities" among team members. But it takes a lot of training to be good at CRM. He notes, "These are not soft skills. They are human skills. They have more potential to save lives than new medical technologies."

---

8 Matthew Wald, "Plane Crew is Credited for Nimble Reaction," *The New York Times*, January 15, 2009.

Ori and Rom Brafman explain more of the rationale for CRM in their book *Sway*, quoting psychologist Barbara Kanki about the way the airline industry used to work. In essence, each pilot was an independent actor, using his personal judgment, intuition, creativity, and experience in deciding how to fly his plane. There was consequently a huge degree of variation. Some pilots would fly around storms, some would fly through them, and some would choose not to fly at all. In addition, the pilot was God in the cockpit. The job of the crew members—no matter their experience or what they had witnessed—was to say, "Roger," and follow the pilot's orders. They were not expected to make suggestions without being asked, even in life-or-death situations, such as an approaching mountain. Were they to do so, the best response they could expect was to be ignored. But, more likely, they could anticipate getting chewed out and having bad marks on their employment record.

The result, as Kanki noticed, could be fatal:

> You had a plane crash because ... the pilot flew into the mountain—not exploring what was underneath the problem.

Southwest Airlines captain Lex Brockington is quoted in *Sway*:

> In the airline industry there was a time when the captain was almighty, in charge of everything, almost godlike. The captain was making a decision and everyone else was scared to overrule him and wouldn't open their mouths.

The Brafmans continue:

The question of how a crew ended up in such disastrous situations intrigued Kanki. When researchers evaluated pilot performance ... they found that "performance differences did not seem to be tied to technical skills. It seemed more to do with management skills."

The industry ultimately came to make huge investments in CRM, creating a cockpit environment in which each person was encouraged, empowered, and expected to participate in critical decisions and situations. All of the members of the cockpit had to learn new means of communication. Pilots had to learn to respond respectfully and promptly when a member of the crew brought up a concern. Crew members, for their part, had to be trained to overcome many years of fear and reticence in bringing up issues. This took months of intensive classwork and simulations, as well as a new personnel management system that evaluated an individual's performance with regard to the new ethic. Pilots who were unable to adapt washed out.

Brockington elaborated on the change in the team dynamic that came about as CRM was institutionalized in this field:

Now, the captain is still ultimately in charge of the airplane. But nowadays it's not like the captain is God.

In fact, when crew members spot a departure from safety procedures, they are trained to challenge the captain. In the CRM method, this occurs in three steps: The first step is to state the facts. If that is ineffective, the next step is to verbally challenge the captain. Finally, if that fails, the third step is to take an action that impedes the ability of the captain to make a fatal error. The Brafmans note, "More often than not, the first two steps are enough to get a captain's attention. The training emphasizes the need for the [crew member] to speak up and for the person in charge to listen and communicate effectively."[9]

While he was not referring to CRM *per se*, MIT Management Professor Edgar H. Schein has described the communications ethic inherent in CRM as follows:

> Team members have to learn how to analyze and critique their own and each other's task performance without threatening each other's face or humiliating each other. That means that subordinates have to learn how to tell potentially negative things to their superiors, and superiors have to learn how to not punish their subordinates for telling the truth if that truth is inconvenient. That, in turn, requires the ability to give and receive feedback in a constructive manner.[10]

You can see how this kind of training would have been valuable and probably would have helped us avoid our embarrassing and harmful wrong-site surgery case. With a CRM-trained team, there is virtually no way the surgeon could have begun surgery without a time out. Everybody in the OR would have felt empowered to say, "Wait, did we check to see that we are about to operate on the correct leg?"

---

[9] Brafman, Ori and Rom, *Sway*. Broadway Books, New York. 2008. pp. 163–166.

[10] Schein, Edgar H., *Helping, How to Offer, Give, and Receive Help*, Barrett-Kohler Publishers, Inc. San Francisco. 2009. Page 118.

I am sad to say, though, that this sort of training program hadn't been implemented in our surgical ORs prior to the incident, despite the fact that it was known about and practiced elsewhere at Beth Israel Deaconess Medical Center.

How Leadership Can Fail

Just three years before the wrong-side surgery case, doctors, nurses, and other personnel in the obstetrics department in our hospital spent months learning CRM after an incident that left a baby dead and a mother near-dead for weeks. The case was devastating and shocking to our staff members, who had always viewed themselves as having one of the best obstetrics departments in the nation. As Barbara Kanki would have noted without surprise, those reviewing the case quickly diagnosed that poor communication among the care team, rather than a lack of technical ability, was the cause of this tragedy. Ben Sachs, the chief of the department, brought in trainers from the Department of Defense to teach his clinicians how to work together in the high-stress "cockpits" of the labor and delivery rooms. The CRM training took many months and was mandatory for all personnel. The result was a substantial improvement in patient outcomes, later documented in peer-reviewed journals.[11]

We received awards for this program, as it was quite innovative in the health care community. Here is the summary of one, the John M. Eisenberg Patient Safety and Quality Award

---

[11] Sachs, Benjamin P., "A 38-Year-Old Woman With Fetal Loss and Hysterectomy" *JAMA*. 2005;294(7):833–840.

issued by the National Quality Forum and the Joint Commission (the national accrediting agency for hospitals):

> This organization is being recognized for the adaptation and application of the military and commercial aviation Crew Resource Management (CRM) principles to the field of obstetrics. After the CRM curriculum was modified for clinical application, 220 staff received training to incorporate the CRM principles and concepts into their daily work processes. The result was a dramatic reduction in major adverse obstetric events, which reduced malpractice liability exposure and improved overall patient safety and the quality of obstetric care. Specifically, a 25.4 percent reduction in the Adverse Outcomes Index (a measure developed for the project) was realized, and the severity of adverse events was reduced by 13.4 percent. The success of this work has been broadly recognized and has driven or influenced similar initiatives, including those of the Harvard Risk Management Foundation, the Commonwealth of Massachusetts, the State of Maryland, and the District of Columbia, among others.

You would think that, based on that experience, we in leadership positions would have encouraged and supported— if not mandated—an expansion of that training program to everybody involved in any kind of surgical or interventional procedure. But we failed to do so, even though the work was "broadly recognized and [drove] or influenced similar initiatives" elsewhere. We therefore ignored a ticking time-bomb, and it was only a matter of time before a process failure would occur in one operating room or another. When it happened, it was more our fault than the surgeon's. If there was anyone to blame, it was I, the CEO, who had failed to assert our obligation to spread what we had learned in the obstetrics department to all the other medical specialties, to every appropriate team of clinicians in the hospital.

I have found that colleagues in other settings have come to similar conclusions.

Paul Wiles, the recently retired President and CEO of Novant Health in Winston-Salem, NC, once told me and a group of hospital CEOs a heart-wrenching story about an infant's death from sepsis in his hospital, which was tracked to an MRSA (antibiotic-resistant staph) infection. The infection was part of a spread of a bug in his neo-natal intensive care unit (NICU) that reached 18 infants in all and may have contributed to the deaths of two others. "This was a direct result of staff not washing their hands appropriately," he said. Since that event, "We have been on a relentless hand hygiene campaign."

The crux of his entire presentation was this comment: "My objective today is to confess. 'I am accountable for those unnecessary deaths in the NICU. It is my responsibility to establish a culture of safety. I had inadvertently relinquished those duties,'" he noted, by focusing instead on the traditional set of executive duties (financial, planning, and such).

Wiles ended his talk to the CEOs in the audience, saying, "If you cannot see the face of your own relative in a patient, or if you cannot see the face of your own son or daughter in the face of a distraught nurse or doctor who has made an error, I suggest that your executive talents would be better placed in other industries."

But it is not just leaders in the hospital world who have come to these conclusions. Let's head to an oil rig in the North Sea.

Death in the North Sea: Leaders Take Ownership

At BIDMC, we learned that the leadership's role in such matters is determinative of process improvement in the organization. Equally important, it also empowers the personal and professional growth of people in the firm. Let me bring in an example from another field, oil exploration, one of the most dangerous occupations in the world.

A number of years ago, Tom Botts was involved in a tragedy aboard an oil rig in which he personally had to call off the search for men missing at sea. Deeply shaken, when he later moved on to be Executive Vice President for Shell Oil Company's exploration and production activities in Europe, he decided that he would implement the most comprehensive program possible  to protect workers' safety at these remote outposts in the ocean. Notwithstanding that new program—the best in the industry—two men lost their lives on a North Sea oil rig when they mistakenly went into a portion of the facility that should have been off-limits. It would have been easy to blame the two men who, after all, entered a prohibited area. Instead, Tom launched a thorough, top-to-bottom review of the organization. He explained:

> We decided to be as open and transparent about the incident as possible and went through a "Deep Learning" journey involving hundreds of people that examined in detail all the root causes that contributed to the accident to get a clear picture of the system that produced the fatalities. Even though the two men who were killed could have made better decisions, my senior leadership team and I could find places where we 'owned' the system that led to the tragedy.
>
> It was a defining moment for us when we, as senior leaders, were finally able to identify our own decisions and our own part in the system (however well intended) that contributed to the fatalities. That gave license to others deeper in the organization to go through the same reflection and find their own part in the system, even though they weren't directly involved in the incident.

Botts wrote me about this incident in response to what happened at Beth Israel Deaconess. He offered an elegant summation of why this kind of approach is important for a leader:

> Thanks for having the courage and commitment as a senior leader of a large organization to role model open and honest dialogue when a mistake is made. Surely that is the best way to ensure learning takes place and improve the chances of the same mistake not being made in the future.

I am a senior executive in the oil and gas industry, and we work incredibly hard to ensure our operations are safe, every day. But sometimes mistakes are made and we have to be aware of systems and behaviors that discourage open and honest dialogue (people fearing there is more to lose than gain by being open). The short term result of transparency is often a lot of second-guessing and finger pointing. But it's important we break through those barriers, as you are doing, and decide to stay focused on the longer term goal of learning and preventing future mistakes.

Once you take that step of committing to transparency and learning, it sets a high bar and it is very hard (probably impossible) to take it back. This approach has helped make us stronger and more aware of the impact of our daily decisions. I wish you full success in your learning journey and encourage you to stick with it!

Is There a Moral Component to Transparency?

We can apply this on a very personal level as we think about our soccer player, Tovah, and consider the impact that my comments had on her life. Yes, her life. Do you remember her saying, 14 years later, "That season was very meaningful to

me?" She elaborated by telling me that my approach to her error had taught her a great lesson, one that she was conscious of trying to apply in her personal and professional interactions today. She is now trying to "pay it forward," offering others the same environment within which to improve.

Tovah today

But we do an incomplete analysis in the context of a company or other institution if we just think of one player. As noted, part of the learning process in an organization and the process of personal development is not only a just, or no-blame, culture. Transparency—willingness to share errors widely—helps create a learning environment that enables process improvement. As a leader this is a key part of your role with regard to creating effective teams. Recall what Tom Botts said:

> But it's important we break through those barriers, as you are doing, and decide to stay focused on the longer term goal of learning and preventing future mistakes. Once you take that step of committing to transparency and learning, it sets a high bar.

In other words, in an organization, the learning and growth process is dependent on the transparency with which the leader makes such learning opportunities available to the entire organization.

Daniel Goleman and his colleagues Richard Boyatzis and Annie McKee consider transparency to be an essential component of inspirational, or visionary, leadership, noting:

> Transparency means the removal of barriers or smokescreens within the company. It's a movement towards honesty and toward sharing information and knowledge so that people at

all levels of the company feel included and able to make the best possible decisions.[12]

But should we not go further? Author Charles Kenney, who has studied and written deeply about process improvement in hospitals,[13] once asked me:

> Isn't there a compelling —perhaps even overriding—-moral component to transparency?

My reply was short and sure, although I was focused mainly on the issue of improving the quality and safety of clinical care:

> The answer, of course, is yes. Doctors and others pledge to do no harm. How can you be sure you are living by that oath if you are unwilling to acknowledge how well you are actually doing the job? As scientists, how can you test to see if you are making improvements in evidence-based care if you cannot validate the "prior" against which you are testing a new hypothesis? At the most personal, ethical level, how can you be sure you are doing the best for people who have entrusted their lives to you if you are not willing to be open on these matters?

But what if you don't work in a hospital? Does it make you uncomfortable to think, as leader, that you have a moral obligation to the principles we have discussed here?

---

[12] Goleman, Daniel, and Richard Boyatzis and Annie McKee, *Primal Leadership, Realizing the Power of Emotional Intelligence*, Harvard Business School Press, 2002, Pg. 58.
[13] Kenney, Charles, *The Best Practice*, Public Affairs, 2008.

Warren Bennis joins Goleman and James O'Toole in suggesting:

> Transparency is one evidence of an organization's moral
> health ... not just a virtuous policy that makes the organ-
> ization feel good about itself, like generous parental leave...[14]

Paul O'Neill, the CEO of Alcoa, thought the moral component was important. He set a corporate goal of eliminating
work-related injuries in his company, all the way from the
mining of bauxite through the processing of finished
aluminum products. He was driven by a belief that this was
the right thing to do for his employees. This belief led to a
series of management standards, full reporting of any and all
injuries, root cause analyses, and process improvements that
changed the nature of his firm. Besides eliminating accidents,
the result was increased efficiency, lower costs, higher quality,
growth in market share, and increased profitability for the
firm. It is noteworthy that his approach relied on recognizing
that personal dignity was inherent to the learning process.

I mentioned one of Mr. O'Neill's goals in Chapter 1. Here it is
again, along with two others he framed as essential questions,
to which every leader should be able to answer "Yes!"

- Are my staff members treated with dignity and respect
  by everyone, regardless of role or rank in the organization?

---

[14] Bennis, Warren, and Daniel Goleman and James O'Toole, *Transparency,*
How Leaders Create a Culture of Candor, Jossey-Bass, San Francisco, 2008.
Pp.42–43.

- Are they given the knowledge, tools and support they need in order to make a contribution to our organization and that add meaning to their life?

- Are they recognized for their contribution?[15]

He then noted that such a leader "causes the creation of an institution-wide system of continuous learning and continuous improvement that engages every employee as part of the problem solving team. Necessary conditions for such a system to work are: real-time identification of everything gone wrong; an associated root cause problem solving process and institution-wide sharing of problems identified and solutions implemented. Total transparency is an essential element of this process."[16]

Is this morality, or just sound business? I want to suggest to you that the two are tied and mutually supportive. Dr. Lachlan Forrow, an ethicist at BIDMC, used to advise me, "CEO stands for Chief Ethics Officer." Note the kinship between Mr. O'Neill's three questions and the "Golden Rule" that is inherent in most of the world's great religions. That is no accident. The level of empathy involved in understanding how your team learns requires a deep and abiding belief in the worthiness of people and an understanding of their values. This is not demonstrable as a business technique you picked

---

[15] http://runningahospital.blogspot.com/2009/12/steps-to-change-culture.html

[16] O'Neill, Paul, "The Key Leadership Behaviors in a Lean Organization," ThedaCare Center for Healthcare Value, http://networkedblogs.com/ol8i9

up in a class at management school: It is a statement of values that is intimately tied to the morality of human society.

CHAPTER 3

"I don't want to be on that team!"

TRIBES MATTER, BUT USE THEM WISELY.

We all have *those* days when coaching a group of girls. They arrive at practice tired from school or last night's sleepover party, and you just can't get them to pay attention or devote as much energy as they should to the exercises of the day.

Over the years, I've discovered a quick solution. I pull out the pinnies (colored vests) and assign half the girls to wear green and the rest to wear red. Then I suggest a competitive game of some sort. Soon, the kids start running, attacking, screaming, and laughing. What's going on?

People have some kind of innate—perhaps Darwinian— tendency toward tribalism. When teams are designated, even drawn from the same cadre, competitive forces come to the fore. Just try to switch one of the girls from red to green after five minutes. "I don't want to be on *that* team!" she will announce, having established a loyalty that clearly has no substantive basis. It is amazing how quickly an "us-versus-them" mentality takes hold.

This can be a powerful force for good in a firm. There are ways to use it to motivate and encourage your staff. Conversely, if unchecked, it can lead to major problems.

Given the nature of organizations, most have teams. These are departments, divisions, or sections of staff focused on one or another set of operations, products, or services within the organization. They are generally necessary and beneficial. However, given the tendency toward tribalism, they also present a potentially detrimental us-versus-them mentality that can create an emotional separation of a team from the organization's priorities, goals, and even values. It's up to you as the leader to recognize when this has happened or might happen and to derail it while finding ways to take full advantage of the good that comes through building teams.

Tribalism Gone Awry: The Nut Island Effect

Teams are more likely to go awry when leaders are not aware or paying attention. This phenomenon can occur when leaders are distracted by other pressing issues, or when leadership attention is missing because a group appears to be performing well enough on its own.

An extreme example developed at the Massachusetts Water Resource Authority, starting before I became executive director in 1987. The case I will describe here helps identify the steps that lead to the formation of the sort of group dynamic that occurs when a team starts to drift from the organization's core mission. The story also offers some insights into how to avoid this kind of situation.

At the time, the MWRA, the agency that oversees the water supply and wastewater treatment for about two million people in the Boston metropolitan area, had a staff comprising 1600 people. A small subset worked at the Nut Island sewage treatment plant adjacent to the Quincy Bay section of Boston Harbor.

Nut Island sewage treatment plant (Courtesy, MWRA)

At this plant, a team of skilled and dedicated employees became isolated from distracted top managers, resulting in a catastrophic loss of ability to perform an important mission, preventing the pollution of Boston Harbor. The irony was that from the outside, the team had all the attributes of an ideal working group: dedication, collaboration, a strong sense of integrity and values, and indefatigable energy with regard to doing the job. It is probably no coincidence that many of the staff members had served in the military, where those virtues were highly valued. Nevertheless, they were failing to do their job correctly. Rather than appropriately treating wastewater and releasing cleaned effluent into the bay, the plant's operating team, despite its best intentions, regularly released untreated or improperly treated sewerage into those receiving waters.

It had become a priority among the Nut Islanders to avoid contact with upper management whenever possible. The employees had set up their own team without the direction and guidance of management. Indeed, they viewed senior management as a common adversary. Nut Island was *their* plant, and its continued operation was solely the result of their own heroic efforts. No bureaucrat in Boston was going to stop them from running it the way it ought to be run.

This isolation led to a lack of accountability with regard to the strategic objectives of the MWRA. It also precluded an infusion of new ideas and approaches, so that the team relied on a stock of ideas limited to those of its own members. The group began to make up its own rules, rules that were terribly insidious because they fostered within the team the mistaken belief that its operations were running smoothly. At Nut Island, the rules actually resulted in improper operation of the plant, especially under extreme weather conditions. The result was increased pollution of the harbor as a whole.

The manner in which team members deluded themselves was complicated, based in part on wishful thinking. It included engaging in strenuous denial when outsiders pointed out inconvenient facts. What was it that caused the team to go underground?

As I reviewed the kind of situation that arose at Nut Island, I found that I could generalize a five-step process that defines the scenario that progressively leads to management-employee alienation, employee self-regulation of critical processes, and finally catastrophic mission failure. In summary, the steps are:

- The senior leadership, focused on high-visibility problems elsewhere in the organization, assigns an important, but behind-the-scenes, task to a team and gives that team a great deal of autonomy. The team members self-select other members based on a strong work ethic and an aversion to the spotlight. They become adept at organizing and managing themselves, and the unit develops a proud and distinct identity.

- The senior leadership takes the team's self-sufficiency for granted. Indeed, the unit may be viewed as an exemplar of "team spirit." At the same time, team members are ignored when they ask for help or try to warn of impending trouble. Then, when trouble strikes, the team feels betrayed by management and becomes resentful.

- As a result, an us-against-the-world mentality takes hold in the team, along with a heightened sense of being a band of heroic outcasts. Now, the team grows skillful at disguising its problems, driven by a desire to stay off the radar screen of the senior leadership.

Team members never acknowledge problems to outsiders or ask them for help.

- Senior leadership, for its part, is more than happy to assume that the team's silence means that all is well. Since senior leadership is failing in its responsibility to expose the team to external perspectives and practices, the team begins to make up its own rules and to tell itself that the rules enable it to fulfill its mission. In fact, though, these rules mask grave deficiencies in the team's performance.

- Both sides, senior leadership and the team, form distorted pictures of reality that are very difficult to correct. They shun one another until some external event, often a catastrophe, breaks the stalemate.

I coined the term "Nut Island Effect" for a *Harvard Business Review*[17]article to describe this kind of situation. The story stimulated dozens of notes from people in many lines of business, noting the existence of the Nut Island Effect in their own firms or institutions. They often wondered what they could do to avoid the syndrome. After all, we cherish and celebrate heroes acting in tight-knit, dedicated teams like those in a World War II movie taking a hill or nabbing an enemy submarine—but we want to make sure they are fighting the right war.

---

[17] "The Nut Island Effect: When Good Teams Go Wrong," *Harvard Business Review*, Volume 79, Number 3. March 2001.

It is far better to be alert to the possibility of the Nut Island Effect and take actions to forestall it before it gets embedded into the corporate culture. But we need to walk a fine line here. After all, the humane values, mission-orientation, and sense of community and commitment that are displayed by tight-knit teams are certainly to be encouraged. How do we support those attributes while avoiding the destructive ones that can arise?

Building Successful Tribes: Going to Gemba

In the case of Nut Island, as with many such cases, the problem starts with isolation. This occurs not only because groups are left alone but also because they *feel* they are left alone. In a world of electronic and social media, some corporate leaders fall into the trap of thinking that global emails and blogs create company-wide community and impart useful information. These can be helpful tools, but they fail in certain respects. First, not everyone reads these missives. Second, not everyone reads them all the way through. Third, words on a computer screen generally do not leave a memorable impression. Finally, even when replies are "allowed," most staff will not reply or offer their own thoughts on the message.

When John Maeda took on the job of President of the Rhode Island School of Design, he committed himself to an extraordinary amount of electronic communication with his community. But he found that this was not always the most effective way to proceed, as he notes in his book, *Redesigning Leadership*:

Traditional broadcast means of communicating, such ... as a campus-wide email, [are] sometimes necessary, but what I've become more and more enamored of is the simplicity of a conversation between two people. It is high-bandwidth, engaging, interactive, and, putting my fiscal hat on for a moment, "expensive." Yet, I've discovered it's the greatest tool that a leader really has.[18]

Much is made of a walking-around style of leadership, and there is a reason for that. Maeda quotes an interim head of RISD, Louis Fazzano: "It's the only way to feel the whole system ... and also to be felt."[19]

To help subgroups avoid isolation, leaders need to find opportunities to be physically present where the teams work. In health care there is a movement to adopt the Lean process, a management system designed to improve patient safety and quality of care by reducing waste and inefficiency in an organization. Lean is based on the principles of the Toyota Production System, a management philosophy that is centered around empowering front-line staff to call out problems and opportunities as they see them. Since this requires an in-depth understanding of what is occurring in the company, those of us who are proponents of the Lean approach talk about the essential value of leaders going to *gemba*. *Gemba* is "the place where work is done"—the factory floor, the loading dock, the

[18] John Maeda, *Redesigning Leadership*, MIT Press. Cambridge, MA. 2011. Page 31.
[19] Ibid, Page 12.

call center, the office, the operating room, the sewage treatment plant.

John Shook, Chairman and CEO of the Lean Enterprise Institute (LEI), explains:

> Gemba ... means "actual place" in Japanese. Lean thinkers use the term to mean real place or real thing, or place of value creation. [Gemba] is where you go to understand work and to lead. It's also where you go to learn.[20]

Lean Enterprise Institute's Jim Womack and John Shook

LEI co-founder Jim Womack continues:

> Gemba. What a wonderful word. The place—any place in any organization—where humans create value.

---

[20] Jim Womack, *Gemba Walks*, Lean Enterprise Institute. Cambridge, MA. 2011. Page vii.

How do we make it a better place — one where we can create more value with less waste, variation, and overburden?

I've been thinking about these questions for many years, and learned long ago that the first step is to take a walk and understand the current condition. Go see, ask why, show respect.[21]

Let's note the mutuality of purpose. Yes, going to *gemba* helps reduce the isolation of a team that might fall into the Nut Island trap, but it also acts to instruct the leader as to what is important to the staff on the front line. It creates a comfortable mechanism for the staff to call out problems, to suggest creative new approaches, to indicate their concerns, fears, and aspirations.

Gemba goes even deeper than that. When Shook and Womack talk about creating value, they do not mean creating value only for the customers of the firm. They posit that creating value also applies to the individuals who work in the firm. This is a matter of worth beyond salary and benefits: It is the value associated with personal and professional growth, with contributing to the greater good, and with relationships among the staff and between the staff and the broader community.

Bringing us back to the theme of this book, your job as leader is not to do. It is to coach. A wonderful example arises in the hospitality and tourism industry. The leaders of the Gaylord

---

[21] Ibid, page xix.

Palms Resort and Convention Center in Kissimmee, Florida, devote themselves to their "STARS," the employees of the organization. Their premise is that an engaged, trained, and competent staff working in a fun-filled environment will be happy and will keep their customers happy and coming back for repeat business. Training manager Richard Caines explained that the Gaylord Palms tries to create an environment to which the staff members love coming every day. He asks, "Now, who does this? Our leaders are responsible for doing this. Notice that I am not using the word manager. We believe managers micro-manage. Leaders lead people. They coach."[22]

Robert Greenleaf expands on this idea using the concept of "servant leadership:"

> The servant-leader is servant first. ... It begins with the natural feeling that one wants to serve, to serve first. Then conscious choice brings one to aspire to lead. That person is sharply different from one who is leader first. ... The difference manifests itself in the care taken by the servant first to make sure that other people's highest priority needs are being served. The best test, and a difficult one to administer, is: Do those served grow as persons? Do they, while being served,

---

[22] http://runningahospital.blogspot.com/2011/12/lessons-for-hospitals-from-gaylord.html

become healthier, wiser, freer, more autonomous, more likely themselves to become servants?[23]

What a virtuous cycle we create when we go to *gemba*! As leaders, we help avoid the isolation that can lead hard-working, well-intentioned teams to be victims of the Nut Island Effect. We gain understanding of our own shop. We stimulate problem-solving creativity that inures to the benefit of the entire corporation. And we help people grow and develop and be more fulfilled members of their community. No wonder Womack calls it a "wonderful word."

"Mr. Ness, everybody knows where the booze is." Get Out of the C-Suite.

I am going to keep you here reading about *gemba* for a while because it is such an important concept that gets to the heart of good leadership. You cannot be properly respectful of your workforce and you cannot be an empathic coach if you do not experience what the team experiences, in real time and on the "factory floor." Likewise, they will not be respectful of you or believe in your desire to be helpful if you don't go to *gemba*. Nut Island was an extreme example of isolation, but degrees of the Nut Island Effect will develop in any organization if the leader allows a gap to grow between his or her own experience and the experience of the staff.

---

23 Greenleaf Center for Servant Leadership, quoting Robert K Greenleaf, "The Servant as Leader." 1970.
   http://www.greenleaf.org/whatissl/index.html

To demonstrate the contrast between the bad and the good, let me present two stories. The first is from a major academic medical center in the United States. The second is from the control room of the regional electric power grid in New England.

A quality-driven MD colleague from Ohio wrote me in frustration about the hospital's chief nursing officer. One day, the CNO asked why there had not been more progress made with regard to reducing the number of central line infections in the ICUs. She didn't know, though, that there had been meetings with the bedside staff which identified a number of problematic workarounds the staff members had created. Although the team had identified these workarounds, they were limited in what they could do to correct them because decisions about equipment and kits were made based on cost, by other divisions of the hospital removed from the bedside. The CNO was upset because the local folks had not shared with her what they had already done and wanted to know why they hadn't told her about these problems.

My friend summarized:

> I explained that if she wanted to find out what was going on, she need only walk onto the unit and ask.

> This all reminds me of the scene in *The Untouchables*. Elliot Ness talks about busting Al Capone if only he knew where he was making his booze. Sean Connery's character (Jimmy Malone) takes him to a post office across from the police station. Ness can't believe the booze is there. Malone says, "Mr. Ness,

everybody knows where the booze is. The problem isn't finding it, the problem is who wants to cross Capone."

The problem isn't knowing HOW to fix this problem. It's doing what it takes to accomplish that—overruling the lawyers and accountants and doing the hard work to change the culture. This can't happen if the C-suite leads from meeting rooms.

Now, for a contrast, let's go to that electric power grid control room. An organization called ISO-New England is in charge of maintaining a reliable supply of electricity to serve the 14 million people in the six New England states. The electronic brain of the operation is a sophisticated control room in which seven operators determine how more than 300 power plants and 8,000 miles of high voltage transmission lines are going to be deployed to deliver 32,000 megawatts of power to the region. The standard of service is that the region should have no more than one day of major outages in any ten-year period, an exceptionally high reliability standard.

 Peter Brandien, Vice President for System Operations, is the leader of the control room crew. He described to me a near miss that occurred on March 17, 2005. There are three extra-high voltage (EHV) transmission lines that span Connecticut, delivering power from stations in the eastern part of the region to the west. On this day, one of the lines was out of service for routine maintenance. Then, another line went out of service unexpectedly. This left a single EHV line in service. The failure of the remaining EHV line would have resulted in cascading overloads on the underlying high voltage transmis-

sion system, potentially leading to a shut-down of the power delivery system to the entire area west of the Connecticut River Valley—Vermont, Western Massachusetts, and portions of Connecticut. Luckily, it didn't happen, but the slow response by the operators to correct the potential problem alarmed Pete.

Pete might never have realized the extent of the underlying problem of focusing only on the immediate action steps to address the initial contingency without understanding the supplementary actions to secure the system if he didn't spend as much time as he does in *gemba*. He is rarely in his office because he's usually out watching and seeing for himself what is going on. His continual presence on the front lines allowed him to recognize what could have been a major issue. The control room crew had properly considered what to do to keep the third line from overloading when the second line went out of service. But, they had not considered the next contingency: What if the third line itself went down?

He brought all of his crews together for a series of problem-solving charrettes.

"I just started asking questions," Pete told me. "Rather than being in a dictator's role and looking for someone's head to hang, I wanted them to think it through. 'What's lacking in the tools we have at hand for situations like this?' 'What's lacking in our training?' I asked questions to help them get a complete answer."

The guys did the analysis, and they designed a simulator training module to deal with this kind of situation for the future. They were quite proud of that accomplishment.

Pete reinforced their good work, but he felt the near miss that had occurred reflected an even larger issue that the team still hadn't addressed; so he then asked his crew, "But why weren't we prepared? Why didn't our thoughts go to this contingency once the second line went down?"

He related later, "I saw a level of discomfort on their faces because they began to realize that they didn't have complete answers and hadn't designed the retraining to avoid this kind of situation in the future." They went back to work and restructured their protocols.

Peter knows that millions of electricity consumers throughout the New England region are dependent on the judgment of his team and on its ability to learn. He said, "I can't have a bunch of sheep that are waiting for Pete to come up with what to do. I don't want to be thought of as a figurehead. I need them to be thinking on their own."

Recognizing the 24-hour-a-day responsibility of the control room, he says, "I'm not there all the time. If they wait for me, we are getting closer and closer to the day we have a failure."

Tom Botts, at Royal Dutch Shell, once used almost identical words in a note to me:

> It takes tremendous energy and iron will to continue to dig deeper to find out how to continuously improve. But those

organizations that don't commit to that will surely face more heartache in the future. The system we are working in (no matter where we work) is constantly changing— just when we think we have it figured out and "controlled," something new crops up or develops. The only answer is an organization that is constantly curious about what we don't know, what is changing, what are the implications from the change I introduced yesterday. It's a muscle most organizations have yet to develop.

By being present with his team in *gemba,* alert to day-to-day impediments, workarounds, and problems, and training his team to analyze problems, Pete Brandein empowers the team members to plan and react on their own. Six years later, one of the operators, Jeff, recognized the learning process that Pete had helped establish: "The light went off in my head as a result of those questions."

Perhaps that chief nursing officer from the Midwest should spend a day in Pete's control room.

Let's now generalize the lesson by exploring how we broaden the reach of problem-solving teams, making sure we have the right people in the room, and training them on how to eliminate wasteful steps in their process.

Empowering Broader Teams

When I divided my soccer players into green- and red-vested teams, I intentionally was creating competition. While you might want to do that from time to time within your company, your purposes are likely to be better served if you focus instead on mixing things up a bit and look for ways to integrate the existing teams' personnel with people from other parts of the organization.

"Oh gawd," you are now saying, "He wants us to create task forces." Why your skepticism? Because we have all been part of an interdepartmental task force created to deal with a perceived problem. It often fails, and we feel like we have wasted our time. Why? Because senior management decides what the problem is and sets a timetable to fix it. The wrong people are often in the room. The task force draws people away from their "regular" jobs. It is considered irrelevant and boring.

So we need a different model.

MIT's Steve Spear has analyzed firms in many sectors to see what works best in creating effective teamwork across departmental and disciplinary lines. Over the years, Steve has noticed that there is often an anomaly in each market arena: a company that stands out with regard to quality, cost, and customer and worker satisfaction—even though it uses precisely the same raw materials as its competitors:

> Here and there, we see companies and organizations, in and out of the private sector, that manage to stay ahead of the pack for years or even decades at a time. Displaying combinations of speed, agility, responsiveness, and endurance, they see and seize opportunities and, by the time rivals have

responded, the leaders have raced on to further opportunities, leaving competitors in their wake.[24]

As an example, he refers to the health care sector in which I was recently employed:

> There are hospitals that deliver far better care to many more people at far less cost than is typical, even though they are treating the same ailments, using the same medical science, employing people trained at the same institutions, and are subject to the same regulations and payment systems.[25]

Steve provides us with a hint as to how this happens in those anomalously successful firms. First, the leadership of these organizations creates a culture that encourages and empowers people "on the factory floor" to call out problems they see. People are trained to understand that they, being on the front line, are the eyes and ears of the company. They are much more likely than the management to see what is working well and what is not.

Second, the successful firms have a system in place to "swarm" around the problems identified by front-line staff. They create real-time interdepartmental teams to conduct root cause analyses and invent solutions. The teams meet at the site of the problem, witness the work flow, and apply their joint creative and analytic energy to solving the discrete problem as quickly as possible.

---

[24] Steven J. Spear, *Chasing the Rabbit*, McGraw-Hill. 2009. Page xvii.
[25] Ibid, Page xix.

Third, the organizations experiment with the solutions, relying again on the front-line folks to tell them how well they are working to solve the identified problems. They make incremental changes. They don't try to reinvent the whole factory. Trial and error is an acceptable and expected part of the improvement process.

Finally, the companies tell the stories of the resulting improvements throughout the organization. This enables other factory floors to learn of the changes and borrow them. It also creates an atmosphere of constant improvement and staff engagement.

As you can see, while this approach avoids the isolation that leads to the Nut Island Effect, it does more than just eliminate that negative tendency. It creates tremendous positive energy and momentum. It is a system of empowerment and broad-based teamwork that leads to continuous system improvement.

So, let's design our interdepartmental task forces based on call-outs noted during our *gemba* visits. Let's ask the assembled team to do a root-cause analysis of the problem, not months after it is noticed, but in as close to real time as possible. You need people from multiple sections of the company to conduct a full root-cause analysis of systemic problems, design possible solutions, experiment with those solutions, and spread the stories of success throughout the organization.

Moving Away from Tasks and Workarounds to a Thoughtful Systemic Approach

The approach I have outlined above requires a different definition of the "workplace." It means that the leader must consider how to move the organization towards a "designed system." Let me first explain the difference between the two, and then we will turn to the question of how you help make the transformation occur.

In a workplace, well-intentioned employees go about their business, carrying out tasks, and following steps, procedures, and processes that have evolved over the years. They are buffeted by external forces, whether from the marketplace or from government regulators. Internally, too, bureaucratic impediments and other hassles often stand in their way. When people encounter such obstacles to their work, they create workarounds so they can continue with their tasks. Those workarounds, in turn, create layers of inefficiency, leading to ever new generations of obstacles and additional workarounds.

Ironically, inefficient workarounds are often caused by the most dedicated, hard-working staff members. Why? Because they are intensely task oriented. Simply put, they are focused on getting the job done. When something gets in their way, they apply great energy to getting around the problem so they can succeed in their assigned task.

In a designed system, we think in terms of processes rather than tasks, and so we are always looking for ways to improve the process, reduce waste, and enhance the work environment.

To create this type of system, we actually need to map out the many steps that constitute a work flow process. By naming each step and understanding the human and other resources being applied to it, we can understand whether or not it is valuable. We often find that many steps are the result of workarounds that were instituted years ago and no longer bring value. It is not unusual in a Lean analysis of a given process in a firm to find that 60 to 70% of the steps people take to do their jobs are wasteful, adding no value to the production process or to the company's customers.

The orthopaedic clinic at my former hospital provides an example. Like many clinics, the process for seeing patients had evolved over many years and incorporated decades of workarounds and other inefficiencies. The average time for a clinic visit was about *three hours*. You would stand in line waiting to check in, followed by a delay waiting to see a doctor, then sit outside of the imaging room waiting for an X-ray, a further wait to see the doctor again after the X-ray, and so on. The clinic was full of disgruntled patients, cranky front-desk staff, frustrated X-ray technicians, and angry doctors.

With great support from Mark Gebhardt, our chief of orthopaedics, a team was assembled and went to work, aided by our hospital's Lean coordinator and other helpers, mapping out every step in the customer service process. It turns out that there were 50 separate steps involved in taking care of a patient. They labeled each step "value added" or "non–value-added," i.e., whether or not the step contributed to the needs of the patients. The team figured out that of the 50 steps, only 22 were really necessary in carrying out the clinic's service to its customers.

After they had mapped out the steps in their patient service process, the group was able to decide on strategies to eliminate non–value-added steps. Then they put them into practice to test their efficacy towards meeting goals of service quality and/or efficiency.

When we began our review, the average amount of time a patient had to spend getting that X-ray and physician consult was 187 minutes. The Lean team, after its analysis, set a target of reducing the time to 84 minutes. But in practice, the visits lasted 60 minutes or less. That's right: down from more than three hours to just about one.

Of course, patients were happy. The staff was very pleased, too. There were fewer cranky patients at the front desk complaining about long waits. There was more efficient use of X-ray equipment and techs' time. Doctors were able to stay on schedule *all day long*. Moreover, they found they were able to create additional appointment slots because they knew they could stay on schedule.

What was the biggest problem? Patients finished their appointments so quickly that their spouses were nowhere to be found. They were still downstairs at the cafe having a cup of coffee, without enough time to read the whole newspaper!

I hope you can see from this example that this kind of detailed analysis can give staff members and leaders a clear picture of what is actually happening on the hospital/factory floor so that they can design systems and focus on quantifiable means by which they can measure success. It also helps everyone to be transparent with regard to their progress. When obstacles to the given process occur, anyone, regardless of rank in the organization, feels free to take the time to call out those problems and work with their teammates to address them in a systemic fashion. The solutions are based on interdisciplinary participation throughout the firm. Rather than being buffeted by external forces, people at all levels incorporate them into their work processes, focusing still on efficiency, quality, and waste minimization.

At BIDMC, we used these same basic tools and applied the Lean philosophy in many other settings to great success. We avoided isolating behavior and built camaraderie across functional lines and the hierarchy of the organization. We delivered better value to our customers and created a more comfortable and collaborative work environment for our staff. By the way, we also saved money because Lean is essentially all about reducing waste.

Pam Kennedy, the director of contracting for the hospital's cardio-vascular institute, provided a representative summary to the staff in the catheterization laboratory after a work review analysis of the expensive supplies used in diagnostic and interventional cardiology procedures. Note that the "regular work" of the Cath Lab had to proceed while the Lean improvement event was carried out. After all, patients who show up with chest pains need to be treated immediately!

Thank you to all the Cath Lab staff on the Lean Team and the nurses and techs holding down the fort while we are conducting all-day Lean sessions towards finalizing the supply replenishment around the work flow process. The Cath Lab purchased 30% less supplies in FY10 compared to FY09 to support the same amount of actual products used in procedures. The FY10 saving in physician preference items (stents, balloons, and catheters) is close to $1 million. The budgeted stent dollars were reduced from $4.8M in FY10 to $3.8M in FY11. There are more savings to be realized once the supply replenishment process has been fully implemented.

Lean is a contemplated journey with evidence-based sustainable outcomes. The Cath Lab Lean "experiment," although challenging, is working.

An important Lean technique that was used in our orthopaedic clinic, the Cath Lab, and elsewhere is called "mapping the value stream." Dr. John E. Billi leads the Michigan Quality System, the University of Michigan Health System's business strategy to transform clinical, academic, and administrative functions through development and deployment of a uniform quality improvement philosophy. He notes, "It's not the map that's valuable. It's the process of mapping, which produces a shared understanding of the value stream and which enables the front-line team to design improvement experiments together."[26]

---

[26] MIT Webinar: http://techtv.mit.edu/videos/15811-using-lean-thinking-to-transform-a-large-academic-medical-center, December 12, 2011.

But this book is about leadership, as well as the tools and approaches that can be used by teams. Let's now turn to the leadership attributes that make such team learning possible. The first thing we need to understand is that traditional views of hard-driving, all-knowing leadership are inconsistent with the creation of effective teams. Instead, modesty and trust become the watchwords.

Using Teams Effectively Requires Modesty in Leadership and Trust in Your Staff

Do you remember what I said before about those anomalous high-performance firms in each industry, the ones that produce high quality products at lower cost than their competitors, even though they use the same production inputs? Steve Spear noted key aspects of these firms. They managed:

> exceptionally complex work that mustered the hands and minds of hundreds of people so that improvement, innovation and adaptation were constant. The factory was not only a place to produce physical products, it was also a place to learn how to produce those products and—most important of all— it was a place to keep learning how to produce those products. … [L]earning and discovery were intrinsic to success.
>
> Such mastery is never complete—it can never be designed into the operation from the start.[27]

---

[27] Spear, op. cit., pages 15–16.

I need to make a very important point about this approach to institutional learning and improvement. It requires incredible modesty on the part of a leader to think about your firm in this way. You have to eschew the idea that you know what will work best for the company in terms of producing its set of goods and services. Just as the Communist government in the USSR was incapable of designing an economic system that would efficiently and rationally produce the needs of a huge country, you, too, are incapable of designing a production or delivery system that will efficiently produce high quality products or services for your customers. Instead, your job is to help create an environment in which quality improvement is a never-ending goal, and one in which every staff member feels empowered to participate and make a part of his or her everyday life.

In our clinic example, neither the chief of orthopaedics nor I knew what the right solution would be to reduce the time spent by a patient needing an X-ray. And, imagine if we had directed the staff to reduce visit times by 66%, from three hours to one hour. All we would have done would have been to raise fear and resentment. Instead of provoking creativity and enthusiasm and communication, we would have generated a collective and emphatic bureaucratic, "No way!" Instead, we admitted at the start that we did not know what the goal would be and how to get there. We had to say to the Lean group, "We trust your judgment. You get to set the performance standard. Tell us along the way what help you need from us to get the job done."

This view is almost heretical among corporate managers who spend a lot of time trying to hold their staff accountable.

They think that because they will be held accountable by their board or the stock market, they need to push along that pressure to the staff. Indeed when I first wrote "The Nut Island Effect," I fell into that trap. I wrote that a way to avoid the Nut Island syndrome was to "install performance measures and reward structures tied to both internal operations and companywide goals."

I don't deny that it is useful to employ performance review systems that contain metrics relating to the individual business unit as well as to the firm as a whole, but what I did not understand back then was that the most effective way to hold people accountable is to allow them to hold themselves accountable. This is inherent in the firms that have adopted the model documented by Steve Spear. At Cincinnati Children's Hospital, they put it this way: "We will be the best at getting better."[28] Author Charles Kenney has studied improvement processes in hospitals and notes:

> The question for so many of these organizations is this: What is the formula for success in quality improvement? ... It is marked by years and years of work. Most of all—more important than anything else—it is marked by leadership, persistence, and a passion to improve.[29]

I find that it can be illustrative to look at the contrary view. Many business writers assert that strict guidelines and

[28] Charles Kenney, *The Best Practice*, Public Affairs. Philadelphia. 2008. Page 125.
[29] Ibid, Page 160.

performance reviews are underutilized, stating most organizations don't make people accountable *enough*.

As you can see by now, I have come to a conclusion about accountability that is at variance with this kind of management guidance on the subject. That guidance suggests that a successful organization depends on holding people accountable to do good quality work in support of corporate objectives. I assert instead that it is not only impossible to hold people accountable in an organization, but trying to do so is a misallocation of a leader's attention.

You say, "What? How will you make sure people are performing up to spec if you don't hold them accountable?"

I view the job quite differently. I view the leader's job as helping to create an environment in which people are given the right tools for doing their jobs and are so comfortable with their roles in the organization that they hold themselves accountable. After all, as I have noted, most people want to do well in their jobs and want to do good in fulfilling the values of the enterprise. Why not trust in their inherent desire to be successful personally and collectively? Instead of focusing on measuring their performance against static metrics, why not create a setting in which they use their native intelligence, creativity, and enthusiasm to solve problems in an inevitably changing environment? Jack Billi likes to point out that this creates "pull-based authority." Empowered by a broad consensus on objectives and the desire to engage in process improvement, the front-line team members are able to exercise their discretion in how to carry out experiments. In short, give them the chance to learn tools that enable them to meet a high standard, both individually and as a team. Then, spend your time praising them and making sure they get credit.

This whole book is about analogies between leading an organization and coaching a girls' soccer team. So, coach, as you prepare your team to play against the outside world, are you prepared to let go, to create an environment in which they are engaged in a continuous learning process? In this chapter, we have talked about the problem of tribes within your organizations, teams that, like the crew at Nut Island, have become dysfunctional through isolation, distrust, and resentment. Shook, Womack, and Spear have shown us the role of leadership in going to *gemba* and structuring an organization that encourages, empowers, and relies on front-line workers to stimulate focused, real-time interdisciplinary approaches to process improvement. We seek to break down the Nut Island Effect and replace it with something glowing and engaging. As Peter Brandein from the electric power control room understood, your personal engagement is essential but, paradoxically, both hands-on and hands-off. As I noted at the outset, your role of coach is not to do, but to enable others to do, to grow and learn personally and professionally, and ultimately to hold themselves accountable to a standard that is consistent with their underlying values and those of the firm. Let's now go and explore in the next chapters how you can succeed with a hands-off approach.

CHAPTER 4

"Why don't you yell at the girls?"

GETTING PAST BLAME.

It was a crisp, lovely autumn New England day, the kind of day that brings out rosy cheeks and giggles among 12-year-old girls playing soccer. At halftime, a father of one of the children, came up to me and remarked, "I notice that you don't yell at the girls when they make mistakes."

I replied, "Huh?"

"During the game, why don't you criticize them on the field when they do something wrong?"

To me, the answer was obvious. First of all, these are 12-year-old girls who choose to play soccer because they love the game and they love to be among their friends. They are also at the age where they take great pleasure in getting better as players. "They know when they've made a mistake," I explained to the father, "Why do they need me to point it out to them?"

It's not my job to interrupt a player's concentration and cause regret by yelling at her after she makes a mistake. There is a better way. It is to wait until she comes off the field and say, "How's it going, Sally?" To which she will respond, "Oh coach, I was trying to do [this move or play], but I flubbed it."

At that point, I ask, "What do you think you would do the next time?" She likely already has a theory of the case and describes how she will handle the situation. If she is correct, I say, "Terrific, try that." If she is mistaken in her diagnosis and remedial approach, I say, "Good idea, but you might also want to think about doing this," and I demonstrate or explain an alternative approach. She knows perfectly well that I am telling her that her way won't work, but it does not come across as a criticism. It feels like a suggestion from someone who cares about her. "OK, coach!" she says.

Next time Sally goes back on the field, a similar situation emerges, and she tries the new approach, and she succeeds. She looks over to me with a broad smile, as if to say, "Look what *I* did!" Or sometimes she doesn't succeed, but at least I have not dampened her enthusiasm and her willingness to try. There will always be more time to work with her on the new skill or tactic. Perhaps it will be in a less pressured environment, like a practice session. Or maybe, something will sink in between this game and the next, and it will work better the next time.

It is in this respect that leading an organization is most like coaching these young girls. To an overwhelming extent, the people in a firm or institution are well-intentioned and want to succeed. As I noted above, they want to do well, and they want to do good. In the vast majority of cases, a person in this environment knows when he or she has made a mistake. You gain nothing—and lose much—if you spend your energy and their time criticizing the error. The idea, instead, is to create a learning environment and use the error as an opportunity for personal growth.

Trained to Blame

The contrast with many professional and corporate environments is evident and sad.

As an example, I offer evidence of the existence and ineffectiveness of this overbearing behavior in the medical community. Linda Pololi is a physician at the Women's Studies Research Center at Brandeis University. She started doing some survey research in the hope of presenting data on the differences that women faculty in medical schools feel from male faculty. While she noted some of those differences, she reached other compelling conclusions highlighting some trends that apply equally to men and women. She presents these in her book, *Changing the Culture of Academic Medicine,* summarizing as follows:[30]

---

[30] Linda H. Pololi, *Changing the Culture of Academic Medicine.* Dartmouth College Press. Hanover, NH. 2010.

We found little indication that medical schools cultivated appreciation of people's efforts. Rather, the focus was on finding fault.

We can easily draw the connection between this and patient care. It is obvious that process improvement is hampered when there is a lack of trust, collegiality, and collaboration among the medical staff. But sadder still, consider the implications for those being treated. Consider, too, how these factors undermine the mission of their organizations. Linda notes:

> There is a parallel between disconnection and emotional detachment among medical school faculty and ineffective communication between doctor and patient. If faculty feel disconnected and cannot communicate among themselves, they are less likely to create good relationships with students and patients. Similarly, in a culture where faculty and administrators themselves do not receive consideration and compassion, it is less likely that they will treat students and patients with compassion.

And what about improving quality and safety and reducing harm to patients?

> Research shows that physicians remember for decades mistakes they have made, feeling guilty and humiliated and isolated in their shame. Only by creating transparency, so they can discuss mistakes openly, can these destructive feelings be relieved. Equally important, open discussion enables the physician and others to learn from these mistakes and prevent them from recurring.

How do you offset the predisposition of most people to want to assign blame, especially when those people are trained professionals, like doctors, whose education supported such an insidious cultural imperative? Or putting it another way, how do you help people in an organization enjoy learning from mistakes? Better yet, how do you get them to recognize near misses—events that occur ten or a hundred times more often than errors—and take pleasure in learning from those signals of systemic problems?

Hospitals are hotbeds of errors and near misses, so they offer us excellent laboratories within which to try out and to study different approaches to creating a learning environment. But, as a scientist might say, the substrate must be appropriate and welcoming. That is a matter both of formal processes and procedures and informal interactions. Let's turn to the formalities first.

A Standard of Justice

If you are going to treat people fairly when errors are made, you need a standard of justice. Continuing our focus on the medical world, many hospitals have adopted guides for making just decisions about behavior. These are often scales based on the nature of the event and the error. At Beth Israel Deaconess Medical Center, we reviewed the work of James

Reason,[31] and our medical leadership voted on it as a standard of review.

The idea is that there are certain events that are always blame-free and others that are certain to require disciplinary action. In the former category, we have mistakes that are made when there is no policy or process in place, when the person incorrectly interpreted an ambiguous policy or process, or when he or she was actually following the official policy. In contrast, people can expect disciplinary action when they intentionally cause harm or tamper with the error reporting process (i.e., engage in a cover-up); when they recklessly or intentionally disregard patient safety; or when they repeatedly violate hospital processes, policies, or standards.

But no chart or formula can cover all events. It is appropriate to acknowledge that judgment will be used in the "gray areas," where someone failed to participate in a patient safety initiative; where the error or near miss resulted from a minor deviation from policy or process; or where carelessness—as opposed to intent—led to a deviation from accepted standards. In evaluating errors within the gray area, we look to see if the act or omission was reckless or repeated, or whether it undermined our patient safety initiatives.

In our hospital and others, this kind of formal template provides comfort to doctors and nurses that there is a standard by which their actions will be judged. Having the

---

[31] Reason JT. *Managing the Risks of Organizational Accidents*. Aldershot, U.K: Ashgate; 1997.

chart is, therefore, a good start. But, we also need to ensure that the judges are judicious in interpreting the standard. Our solution was a multi-level review procedure, starting with department level quality control officers and culminating in reviews by the senior clinical and administrative leadership (Chief of Service, CEO, COO, Chief Nursing Officer) in the most serious cases. We made clear through action and demeanor that such reviews were not Inquisitional trials: They were professional peer-review assessments of the facts and actions that had occurred. It was the professional and amicable conduct of these reviews over the years that signaled to members of our medical staff that they would get a fair shake. The result was an increasing likelihood that mistakes would be admitted and reported and not driven underground.

The Practice of Justice Must Match the Written Standard

Formal processes, though, are not enough in and of themselves. They must be paired with actions and words "on the street"—in this case, on the floors and units of the hospital—or people will learn that "gotcha" is really the rule of the day rather than the ostensible just process. We knew we needed all managers to be on board, both philosophically and operationally, with our approach. In order to cement this buy-in, we engaged in extensive training of nurse managers and other leaders in the organization, encouraging them to welcome the reporting of errors and to use such instances as opportunities for personal and professional growth, as well as for exploring systemic weaknesses in the hospital.

There is an excellent example of this practice in action at another institution in an article by Dr. Charles Denham, in which he relates the practice of nursing chief Jeannette Ives-Erickson, Senior Vice President For Patient Care and Chief Nurse at Massachusetts General Hospital.[32] When there is a screw-up in nursing, she calls the involved nurse into her office and asks one question: "Did you do this on purpose?" When the nurse answers, "No," then Jeannette says, "Well then it is my fault. ... Errors stem from system flaws. ... I am responsible for creating safe systems."

Chuck notes, "In a few short moments with a caregiver after an accident, the leader declares ownership of the systems envelope, and the performance envelope of her caregivers, and creates a healing constructive opportunity to prevent a repeat occurrence."

He warns us that it is easy to "automatically fall in a name-blame-shame cycle, citing violated policies, and ignore the laws of human performance and our responsibility as leaders."

Accordingly, it is the combination of the formal and informal that, over time, establishes the culture of the organization. You may recall the case I mentioned in Chapter 2 about a doctor who was suspended in 2006 for violating one of our hospital's safety regulations.

---

[32] Dr. Charles Denham, "May I have the envelope please." *Journal of Patient Safety*. 2008 Jun;4(2):119–123.

Although there had been no harm to the patient, we disciplined the doctor with a temporary suspension of privileges. The fact that we took this action ended up in the newspapers because we had to report the disciplinary action to state regulators, who make it a matter of public record. This doctor was an expert in his field and very well regarded in the region. He often took on cases that were so difficult that others would refuse to take them.

A number of people in the hospital and from other hospitals contacted me about the case, wondering how we could treat such an exemplary doctor in such a manner. It occurred to me that the situation presented an opportunity to remind everyone in our hospital about our standards and procedures that had been in place for some time but perhaps weren't as widely understood as they should have been. In order to reach the most people, I did so in a direct email to the staff. I summarized the case and then explained exactly why we had penalized such an excellent surgeon.

First, I outlined our formal process:

> Our Medical Executive Committee, comprising all of the departmental Chiefs and several other members of the physician staff, establishes rules of procedure and conduct that apply to medical care professionals here at the hospital. Those rules call for review of major adverse events and near misses whenever they occur. (Given industry experience, we can expect about four to six such episodes each month.) We conduct confidential peer reviews of these cases in the following manner: First, appropriate cases are identified at departmental conferences. These are then reported to our

Department of Health Care Quality, where they are investigated to determine the root cause. We look for ways to learn from them and make improvements so we can better serve our patients. The vast majority of those reviews do not result in punitive action against a doctor. Indeed, we depend on healthcare professionals to disclose fully all facts so that the process can be accurate and helpful to future patients.

And then I made it personal:

No one takes pleasure from a process in which a highly trained physician who has devoted his or her life to healing patients is put through the agony of this kind of publicity. On the other hand, the public has a right to know if a caregiver has acted in a manner inconsistent with the professional standards established by his or her peers. Men and women who choose to become doctors do so out of a great sense of service to their fellow human beings. The fact that we engage in intense review processes of our own colleagues is a sign of this quest for excellence. On those few occasions when a member of the medical staff is hurt or embarrassed by this process, it is because his or her colleagues have acted to prevent patients from potential harm in the future.

As a leader, you can never be sure if a broadcast message like this is going to work. Email is passive and inherently imprecise. You cannot see people's reactions as they read it, if they read it at all. It would be better to have in-person conversations, but the impracticality of that and the need for timeliness sometimes prevails. But you wonder: Will they understand it? Will they agree? In this case, though, I received immediate validation. Later that day, a nurse sent me this note:

I feel inclined to respond to your email with an experience I had today on the floor. At work today I made a mistake, a medication error. My stomach turned, I felt faint … however I recalled my focus earlier in the day: on the integrity of the hospital and the type of light that it shined on my paradigm as I entered my day. I felt an immediate sense of freedom and put my attention on what I needed to do to correct the error. Although embarrassment and fear visited me, I wasn't overwhelmed by the emotions. I contacted the right people, and helped maintain the safety of my patient. It was a very challenging day … and I grew. I will go to sleep with integrity; knowing I was honest, feeling I had done all I could.

I know healthcare presents these types of moral dilemmas to all of us who choose this challenging field to work in. Beth Israel is a safe place to honestly confront these dilemmas and strive to achieve the excellence that I know can exist.[33]

What more powerful confirmation of our approach could one imagine? A scared young nurse makes an error but feels comfortable enough to report it to a supervisor, trusting in our just culture to treat her well, and to learn from the experience. I have to tell you that this was one of the most uplifting moments in my nine years as CEO.

---

[33] http://runningahospital.blogspot.com/2006/10/errors-improvement-and-discipline_19.html

Sad Results from Imposing Blame

Let's contrast this nurse's experience with a case at the University of Pittsburgh Medical Center and another at Seattle Children's Hospital.

I noticed the UPMC case in a newspaper article that began:

> A Pennsylvania medical center demoted a surgeon and suspended a nurse who were involved in the transplant of a kidney from a donor who had hepatitis C, a spokeswoman said on Thursday.

I immediately suspected that this story was not totally a person problem, since the nature of the error suggested instead that there were systemic problems at UPMC that underlay the error.

Sure enough, a follow-on press story said:

> The positive hepatitis C test that was missed at UPMC, leading to the shutdown of its living donor kidney transplant program, was not noticed by its entire transplant team despite a highlighted alert in the hospital's electronic records system.
>
> "Everyone just missed it," a source with knowledge of the case said.
>
> The alert was missed by as many as a half dozen people on the transplant team who typically would have reviewed such a test result, according to interviews with several current or former UPMC employees. A number of those interviewed said the problem lies more with the larger system of ensuring that

medical errors are caught than with the individuals involved in the incident.[34]

And a still more tragic case involved Kimberly Hiatt, a Seattle nurse who committed suicide months after being disciplined for administering a fatal dose of calcium chloride to an infant. Hiatt had worked as a neonatal intensive care unit (NICU) nurse at Seattle Children's Hospital for almost thirty years. By all accounts she was a devoted and highly capable and compassionate nurse. Hiatt was fired soon after the infant's death. Also, soon after the infant's death, the Seattle Hospital changed its policies to require stricter control and checks on the administration of calcium chloride, which is considered an especially dangerous drug in medically fragile infants.

In the *Seattle Times* editorial and opinion pages, F. Norman Hamilton, a retired anesthesiologist, wrote, "The fact that the hospital changed its policies after the death implies that they realized that its policies were inadequate. Despite this, the hospital decided to fire the nurse for an arithmetic error. ... If we fire every person in medicine who makes an error, we will soon have no providers. ... It is my belief that if the nurse had been dealt with appropriately— with compassion and insight—that she, today, would be a valuable and happy nurse."[35]

---

[34] http://m.post-gazette.com/local/region/entire-upmc-transplant-team-missed-hepatitis-alert-1159219?p=0

[35] http://seattletimes.nwsource.com/html/northwestvoices/2014847389_suicideofnurseaftertragicevent.html

Mistakes Are Good

Let's go back to the generalizable lesson. In soccer terms, we don't want to yell at or punish players for making mistakes; rather, we want to use those mistakes in a respectful fashion and in an appropriate setting as learning opportunities. We have to teach our subordinates that the public exposure of an error is not an exercise in assigning blame. It is part of our acknowledgement of systemic and human flaws. After all, the last thing we want to do is drive near misses and mistakes underground, where their inherent lessons remain buried. MIT's Steve Spear has addressed this point, while complimenting the approach of our hospital and other like-minded organizations:[36]

> Paul Levy and his colleagues at BIDMC are on exactly the right track in calling out errors, and they are setting an example that should be emulated energetically at other hospitals. Delivering care requires coordinating harmoniously an extraordinary number of individual disciplines. This means anticipating myriad interactions of patient, provider, place, and circumstance, and anticipating perfectly all circumstances is impossible. However, by responding when things go wrong, those working in and responsible for care delivery processes can see their vulnerabilities, identify their causes, and rectify weaknesses, leading to ever improving efficacy, efficiency, and responsiveness. This is not a hypothetical assertion: Order of magnitude improvements in care have been recorded in Pittsburgh hospitals, at Ascension Healthcare and Virginia

---

[36] http://runningahospital.blogspot.com/2011/01/moral-component-to-transparency.html

Mason Medical Center, and elsewhere. Those hospitals not pursuing the same degree of openness are not any less dangerous. They are simply not admitting the reality to themselves, their staff, and their patients.

If Linda Pololi is correct that the training ground of American physicians works against this commonsense view of the world, is there any doubt as to why we have such problems in patient care? What more terrible thing can you say to a doctor than that he or she is not permitted to make mistakes and that he or she will be pilloried for doing so? Clinical and administrative leaders in hospitals must strive to undo the culture that is embedded in these centers of learning and help those who have devoted their lives to alleviating human suffering to start, first, to alleviate their own suffering and sense of loneliness and isolation.

The same applies to any organization. You, as leader, must take the lead in trusting the people with whom you work and creating an environment in which helpful coaching, rather than intemperate criticism, is the expected behavior. If you model that behavior, others will emulate it, and it will become the culture of your organization.

Back to the father of the 12-year old. When I saw him at the next game, he said to me, "On the way home, Suzie said to me, 'Dad, you know something? I play better when I am having fun!'" QED.

CHAPTER 5

"Aren't you taking this a bit too seriously?"

AVOID SELF-DESTRUCTIVE COMPETITION.

 Ali, aged 14, looked like Li'l Orphan Annie. Short, with a head full of curly red hair and freckles, she was refereeing a game of 12-year-old players. One of the coaches, a large middle-aged man, was persistently and angrily yelling from the sidelines about the calls she was making.

She calmly walked over to the coach, looked up at him and said, "Don't you think you are taking this a bit too seriously?"

Abashed, he reddened, apologized, and was calm for the rest of the game.

Another time, I was coaching my daughter's team, a group of 9-year-olds, in Dedham. It was a close game—back and forth, from offense to defense—and nobody could score. Finally, we took a shot. The ball clearly went into the goal, but it bounced against the metal bar at the back of the goal and re-entered the field of play. The youth referee, a 14-year-old boy, did not see this happen. Why? He had stopped running at the other end of the field to tie his shoe, so he was looking down at the ground when the goal was scored, and all he saw, when he looked up, was that the ball was still on the field of play. We went on to lose the game 1–0.

I knew enough not to yell at the boy, but I was furious at the refereeing error. After the game, I got into my car, still steamed up at the injustice and the loss. My daughter Sarah and one of her buddies piled into the back seat. They, too, had seen what happened. But here's the thing: They were already jabbering about other topics, having left the game behind them. To them, it was just a game. They had had fun. Now, off to the next thing.

And yet another time, years later at another tournament, my superb under-12 girls team was in the final match against an equally superb team from another town. We both went into that match undefeated in the previous four games. Indeed, we had scored 16 goals and only allowed in three, but this final contest was much more difficult and intense. It was attack and parry for 50 minutes of the 60 minute game. It was clear that whoever scored first would probably win. The parents and I had our hearts in our mouths for every moment. I would later note to the parents that "it was almost eerie how quiet you all were."

Then, one of the opposing players fell down with an injury. The coach disdainfully and loudly said to her as he walked across the field, "Haven't you been down long enough yet?" My girls and I looked at each other silently. One, standing next to me on the sidelines, said, "Can you believe that guy?" We watched as the other team deflated emotionally. Shoulders dropped. You could see that their girls were standing with their feet flat on the ground, as opposed to being poised lightly on the balls of their feet. Shortly after the play restarted, at minute 55, we scored the first and only goal of the game and walked away with the championship.

The tournament champions!

These girls naturally understood something about competition and its role in the game. Let's acknowledge that a key component of leadership is to demonstrate your own competitive juices to help motivate your organization to beat the other

guys. Competition, after all, is an important force in encouraging excellence, creativity, and teamwork.

But there is a point beyond which a focus on competition is
self-destructive. That point is when you lose perspective,
either about the people in your own organization or about the
competitor. When that happens, you are likely to devote too
much time and other resources in response to the other
organization's perceived tactics and not enough to the
strategies and tactics that are best suited to your own
organization. You also risk objectifying or denigrating the
members of your team, as opposed to trusting them and
relying on their judgment, creativity, and skills in carrying out
your mission. Finally, an over-reliance on competitive fervor
draws energy from your major task as leader, which is helping
to establish an ever more aspirational vision for the
organization.

Avoid Self-Destructive Competition

This concept is central to the teachings of Peter Senge, a
lecturer at MIT's Sloan School of Management who studies
how to decentralize the role of leadership in organizations in
order to enhance the ability of employees to work productive-
ly toward common goals. He also focuses on the managerial
and institutional changes needed to build more sustainable
enterprises, businesses that foster social and natural as well as
economic well-being. In *The Fifth Discipline*, Senge acknowl-
edges the importance of competition, but he also sets forth its
limitations:

Nor is there anything wrong with competition. Competition is one of the best structures yet invented by humankind to allow each of us to bring out the best in each other. But after the competition is over, after the vision has (or has not) been achieved, it is one's sense of purpose that draws you further, that compels you to set a new vision.[37]

This is particularly important when you face competitors with a stronger balance sheet or a reputational advantage in their field. You need to let your team play its own game, based on their underlying set of values and purposes, not the other team's game. While running Beth Israel Deaconess Medical Center, I was sometimes asked, when we were about to make a strategic decision, what the larger and wealthier other Harvard hospitals in Boston were doing in that arena. My reply was, "Do you think Apple cares about what Dell is doing?[38] We are setting our own path. Let's be creative and see how it works. We can make mid-course corrections later. Our competitive advantage is our collaborative ability to be nimble and to be the best at getting better. Besides, we are serving a broader vision here, one that is not measured by our competitors' activities."

But if your primary focus is not on the competition, how do you get better and succeed in the marketplace? First, you have to decide on the purpose you are serving. Next, as Senge

---

[37] Senge, Peter. *The Fifth Discipline*. P. 149.

[38] This was well before many post-death encomiums were written about Steve Jobs and his approach to designing products at Apple.

suggests, you have to create an internal structure that drives your organization to constant improvement.

On Purpose

Let's talk first about purpose. I had a chance once to hear a talk by Roy Spence, the author of *It's Not What You Sell, It's What You Stand For: Why Every Extraordinary Business Is Driven by Purpose.*[39] As suggested by the book's title, his proposition is that truly excellent organizations are those characterized by a common sense of purpose. This is different from having a mission statement or corporate objective, which state a business direction. It is more about having a desire to change the world for the better.

An example Roy gave was Southwest Airlines, whose purpose is to give people the freedom to fly. You can probably quote the tag line: "You are now free to move about the country." I listened as Roy talked about the airline's actualization of this sense of purpose. It happened back in 2009 when nearly the entire airline industry decided to start charging for baggage. Southwest was counseled by its financial advisors that doing the same would not only save millions of dollars but also make millions of dollars by saving money on labor and collecting baggage fees. CEO Gary Kelly decided, though, that charging people for luggage would conflict with the company's purpose, and so—contrary to all advice—he

---

[39] Roy Spence, *It's Not What You Sell, It's What You Stand For: Why Every Extraordinary Business Is Driven by Purpose.* Penguin Group, New York. 2009.

decided not only to keep the free luggage policy but also to launch the now famous *Bags Fly Free* advertising campaign. "We love bags!" proclaimed actual baggage handlers on the tarmac.

Sure enough, the company did not save or make a few millions of dollars from this decision. Instead, the airline increased its share of the domestic market by about 1%, or $800 million to $900 million, as the public responded by shifting gobs of business from other carriers.[40]

I hadn't thought about Roy's talk much until I got on an American Airlines flight a few weeks later and noticed virtually every passenger board a full flight with a rollerboard style suitcase to put in the overhead bins. They were all trying to avoid the $25 fee for checking bags. The tension was palpable among passengers and flight attendants. Passengers who boarded later peered ahead in the aisle wondering if and where there were open spots for their bags. Flight attendants were alternating between repacking each overhead bin to maximize its carrying capacity and hurrying passengers along so we could have an on-time departure.

The result: Airline employees were devoting all of their emotional energy to the baggage. If you had questions about anything else, they could not make eye contact because they were scanning the bins for empty spaces.

---

[40] *USA Today*, http://www.usatoday.com/travel/flights/2009-12-13-southwest-checked-bags_N.htm

Another result: Passengers' relative comfort with the flight had already been diminished, and we hadn't even taken off yet. Class divisions appeared between the "haves" and "have nots." Those of us who arrived earlier (because of priority access) felt the calm superiority of secure overhead bag placement, while those who arrived later felt like they had missed something. One person actually asked me how I had managed to get on board before her.

The contrast between the atmosphere on Southwest and American was all about having a different sense of purpose. For Southwest's staff, everything is about wanting to give us the freedom to fly, and because of that, the airline's customers never have a doubt that the company will do what it can to help them enjoy that freedom.

I realized as I buckled in that I'd be hard-pressed to figure out American Airlines' purpose. I opened up the magazine in the seat pocket to see if I could find it. There was a letter from the CEO that said something about "all my AA colleagues all over the world who put their hearts and souls into taking you wheresoever you want to go in the world." At first blush, you might read that as very close to what Southwest says, but it is not quite the same. The AA line is about what they will do for you; it's not about what you can do for yourself. It is not liberating. It is creating dependence.

What Roy Spence makes clear is that a real purpose can't just be words on paper. "An effective purpose reflects the importance people attach to the company's work. It taps their idealistic motivations and gets at the deeper reasons for an organization's existence beyond just making money. Purpose is a definitive statement about the difference you are trying to make in the world."[41]

At BIDMC, we had a long-standing purpose. It was not a business objective in our strategic plan or mission statement, but it was deeply held: "To treat patients and their families as we would want members of our own family treated." Achieving this purpose was a full-time endeavor for those who worked there—including those involved in research and teaching as well as clinical care.

Beyond Purpose: Execution and Creative Tension

Of course purpose also has to be translated into action, and for that you need to focus on particular key products, services, and metrics that are essential for getting the job done. My colleague in the Boston Harbor Cleanup Project, engineer Richard Fox, had a sign on his desk, "Implementation is everything." As I shall soon discuss, Peter Senge again offers extremely valuable insights. His concept of creative tension is the tool that enables effective execution in a complex organizational environment. Let me explain, again, by using an example from our hospital.

Our particular vision at BIDMC was to make an explicit commitment to improving the quality and safety of care delivered to our patients, to measure our progress in doing so, and to be utterly transparent with regard to those matters to our own staff and to the world at large. You might think that

---

[41] Spence, op. cit, p. 10.

it would go without saying that a hospital should be concerned about quality and safety, but it is the sad truth that these items are not usually given the strategic attention that they deserve. In two important reports in 1999 and 2001, the Institute of Medicine (IOM) documented that 100,000 people were being killed in American hospitals each year because of preventable medical errors.[42] As the IOM notes, "Between the health care we have and the care we could have lies not just a gap, but a chasm." The numbers reported by IOM have stayed remarkably constant since their publication.

Our faculty and administrative leaders, and members of our Board, decided that we should adopt a vision that would reverse these kinds of numbers in our hospital. While we felt that improving our record on this front might help distinguish us from other hospitals in Boston, the main impetus was simply to provide better care to our patients. We had always had the view that our purpose was to "deliver the kind of care we would want for members of our own family," but we realized that we were failing to do that in a systemic and quantifiable manner.

We concluded early on that being transparent about our quality and safety metrics was an important component of achieving success. This was risky business, in that we would be posting our infection rates and other rates of preventable harm for the world to see. What if patients responded by

---

[42] The Institute of Medicine, *To Err Is Human: Building a Safer Health System*, 1999; *Crossing the Quality Chasm: A New Health System for the 21st Century*, 2001.

getting nervous about these problems at our hospital? What if referring physicians in the community decided to send their patients to our competitors instead?

We were convinced that any possible risks inherent in transparency would be overshadowed by its efficacy in fulfilling our vision. We knew that transparency's major value as a strategic imperative is to provide creative tension within a hospital so that staff members hold themselves accountable to the standard of care to which they have jointly agreed. How does this work?

First you, as leader, help the people in your team establish an audacious goal for the organization. The goal has to be clear, measurable, and non-debatable. In sports, this pick is easy, as the goal is usually to win the game or the tournament, and the result is clear by the end of playing time. But for my soccer teams, the goal was not always to win. Early in the season, for example, we set developmental goals that reflected a focus on skill improvement. How many times can we connect three passes in a row? How many times can we accurately head a ball? Let's set a new record for ourselves and try to beat it in the next game.

In a firm, the goal can be any of a number of quantitative metrics. In our hospital, the goal was to eliminate preventable harm. Not to reduce it by 10% per year, but to send it to zero.

Paul O'Neill, the former CEO of Alcoa, explains this concept when he describes what any organization interested in achieving habitual excellence must have:

A leader who articulates and establishes aspirational goals for the institution. By aspiration, we mean goals that are set at the theoretical limit of what is possible. For example, zero nosocomial infections, zero medication errors, zero patient falls, zero work place injuries for all employees, zero wasted time spent hunting and fetching, zero duplicative or repair work for things not done correctly the first time, i.e., lab work or imaging studies. [43]

He expands:

Setting goals at theoretical limits sharpens the understanding of the size of the opportunity relative to current performance. Benchmarking against national averages or even better performers can create the illusion of success or satisfaction with "good enough."

For our hospital, I used to say, with regard to preventable harm, "The target is zero, zilch, nada. No other target is intellectually or morally defensible."

Second, you make the goal public, and you also make public the data indicating your progress toward meeting the goal. The gap between where you are now and your desired end-state is what establishes a creative tension for your organization that drives people to achieve the vision.

---

[43] O'Neill, Paul, "The Key Leadership Behaviors in a Lean Organization," ThedaCare Center for Healthcare Value,
http://networkedblogs.com/ol8i9

For our hospital, I used to say: "Our data are here (on our company website) for the world to see, mainly to help us hold ourselves accountable to the standard of care to which we aspire."

Senge explains:

> [T]he gap between vision and current reality is ... a source of energy. If there was no gap, there would be no need for any action to move toward the vision. Indeed, the gap is the source of creative energy. We call this gap creative tension.
>
> Imagine a rubber band, stretched between your vision and current reality. When stretched, the rubber band creates tension, representing the tension between vision and current reality. What does tension seek? Resolution or release. There are only two possible ways for the tension to resolve itself: pull reality towards the vision or pull the vision towards reality. Which occurs will depend on whether we hold steady to the vision.[44]

And holding ourselves accountable in this manner did work. Our hospital made clear and continued progress in reducing infections, falls, medical errors, and other types of harm to patients. We documented our progress quarterly on our corporate website, for the world to see. Our open approach on these matters brought us a mention from the Massachusetts Senate in 2008, citing our "unparalleled leadership in health care quality and patient safety." We were the subject of

---

[44] Senge, op. cit., p. 150.

numerous articles and case studies around the world,[45] and
were used as an example in conference talks by international
experts in process improvement. Instead of raising concerns
among patients and referring physicians, our approach
generated increased trust in our hospital and our physicians.

The Marketplace Responds

Although we had not intended it to be a competitive factor,
holding true to our purpose and implementing specific
attributes of our vision was the major cause of a decision by
the state's largest multi-specialty physician practice, Atrius
Health, to change its referral patterns. Its CEO, Eugene
Lindsey, called me one day in March, 2009 and said, "We really
like what you are doing with quality and safety improvement
and transparency. It is consistent with our vision for our
practice. Would you have the capacity to take some of our
patients?"

This call was a big deal for us. At a tertiary hospital like ours,
the institution's financial well-being depends on the size and
loyalty of its referral network (i.e., community-based doctors
in primary care and specialty practices who need a reliable and
accommodating hospital to which they will send their patients
needing advanced care). Referral relationships tend to be

---

[45] For example, The Health Foundation in the United Kingdom produced
a case study entitled, "Beth Israel Deaconess Medical Center, How
leadership and a focus on quality rescued Beth Israel Deaconess
Medical Center." November 2010.
http://www.health.org.uk/publications/beth-israel-deaconess-medical-
center/

based on trust first, and then habit. They are long-lasting. Once trust is established, local doctors are not likely to switch hospital allegiance and send their patients to a different place.

In this case, the Atrius organization had been sending its tertiary care patients to another hospital in Boston for over twenty years. Personal relationships between the community doctors and the hospital-based specialists had become cemented during that time. But Gene sensed that there was a disconnect between the perceived purpose of Atrius and its clinical priorities and the mission and clinical priorities of the incumbent hospital. He took a big chance, as leader, in initiating the phone call, knowing that he was dealing with years of established referral patterns.

While Gene and I had an instinctive feeling that this could work out well, it was important to memorialize that our two institutions did, in fact, have a common purpose and clinical priorities. His phone call immediately resulted in planning discussions between our respective clinical and administrative leaders, but it was not until the senior leadership of our two organizations could agree on a joint vision statement that the deal could be consummated. I volunteered to write a first draft because I felt that I could frame the issues in the manner suggested by Roy Spence—looking for idealistic motivations, getting at the deeper reasons for the organization's existence, and setting forth the difference we were trying to make in the world—but also draw on the lessons set so clearly by Paul O'Neill and Peter Senge about creating a self-accountable learning environment, in which every staff member would be valued for his or her participation. Importantly, that vision statement made no mention whatsoever about competitive issues in the marketplace. It was, pure and simple, a codification of mutually held values, respectful of each institution's history but looking to the future.

Here it is, in its entirety. The first section recited the history of the antecedent organizations that then comprised BIDMC and Atrius. This recounting was a way of valuing long-standing staff members and also making clear that the underlying purposes of the two organizations were aligned.

Introduction

When planning for the future, history matters. History embodies culture, experience, and values. It is the application of those to a shared and exciting vision that binds people in a productive and collaborative fashion for the good of society.

As Atrius and Beth Israel Deaconess Medical Center consider a future together, we take the time to be respectful of our past journeys apart, drawing lessons and strength from them. We remember our antecedent institutions and why they were created. Harvard Community Health Plan was designed by some of the medical giants of Boston, people with a vision of patient-centered, managed care delivered in a comfortable and integrated setting. Southboro Medical Group, Granite Medical, Dedham Medical Associates, and South Shore Medical Center were created to provide warm, convenient, family-centered approaches to care delivery with a strong level of collaboration among the doctors in these physician practices. New England Deaconess Hospital was founded by members of the Methodist faith who wanted a place "where science and kindliness unite in combating disease." And Beth Israel

Hospital, born out of discrimination against one religious group, vowed to provide access and equal quality of care regardless of religion, race, or ethnicity, supported by strong research and education programs.

Each of these organizations has been successful by growing and adapting to changes in society and the health care environment, but the underlying values have remained inviolate. Today, each faces a new set of challenges, and we believe they have a better chance of success by facing them together.

Together, though, does not mean corporate mergers or takeovers. It means, instead, a mutually respectful strategic alignment of assets and services in support of the public good. Our shared vision is based on terms that are commonly tossed around but that are often not executed. Our plan is not only to have a vision, but to hold ourselves mutually accountable to a successful implementation of that vision.

The next section set forth a purpose for the future, how we would attempt to make the world better, but drew again on the values of the two organizations. We made explicit mention of many of the specialties in the two organizations, reflecting their importance to a well-functioning and compassionate health care delivery system. Importantly, too, we directly covered implementation of the mission, and which guiding principles and approaches would be employed. We acknowledged that setting audacious goals and transparency would be essential building blocks of our joint venture.

Our Vision

We aim to establish the model health care delivery system in the Commonwealth of Massachusetts. The partners signing this document—and with other like-minded organizations in the state—will offer the public a full spectrum of health care services that are patient-centered, compassionate, integrated, and evidence-based. The heart of our service model will be a strong emphasis on primary care. We believe that prevention and diagnosis and treatment must be based on deep relationships between primary care doctors and families. We believe that primary care doctors must be given the time and resources to understand a patient's personal and medical background, to conduct full evaluations of medical problems, and to supervise the provision of care throughout secondary and tertiary treatment.

We believe that specialists bring tremendous value in their enhanced and detailed expertise in their areas of specialization, but they must work in close cooperation with primary care practices to ensure treatment of the whole patient and not just a particular set of symptoms.

We believe that nurses, technicians, and other allied health professionals are essential members of the health care delivery team and should be integrated into planning each patient's needs.

We commit ourselves to enhancement and further integration of our electronic medical records and computerized decision-support systems in furtherance of providing seamless delivery of care regardless of setting within and across our institutions.

We believe that our organizations have an ethical and moral responsibility to eliminate preventable harm from the health care delivery system, whether in doctors' offices, procedural areas, or hospital floors and units. We believe that it is appropriate and part of a just culture to publicly publish our progress towards this goal.

We believe that an educational and research mission is integral to our vision. Teaching the next generation of health care professionals is not only a societal responsibility, but it also enhances the ability of current providers by helping to ensure that they are up-to-date on the latest scientific and technical advances. Research likewise has broad societal implications, but it also provides current opportunities for clinical trials and other diagnostic and treatment advances for our patients.

We believe that it is our obligation to improve the efficiency of our health care delivery system by the application of the approaches and techniques of continuous process improvement of the type exemplified by the Lean methodology. Our philosophy relies on the concept of empowering every individual in our organizations to call out problems and opportunities in real time, and of requiring managers and supervisors to seriously consider those suggestions and act on them to resolve problems to root cause and disseminate stories of improvement throughout our organizations.

We believe that patient involvement in the design of our process, systems, and facilities is essential to having a patient-centered environment. We will make use of patient advisory councils, secret shoppers, survey instruments and other approaches to enhance our decision-making and delivery of service.

We believe that the business relationships among our partners must be designed to align institutional and personal financial incentives in support of the delivery system we aim to provide. Those relationships must be completely open and transparent to all the partners and based on commonly agreed upon accounting principles. We intend to be financially successful, because we know that future investment in people, modern equipment, and pleasant facilities is a necessary condition of delivering high quality care.

We intend to offer ourselves to insurance companies and self-insured institutions and businesses as the high quality, low cost provider network in the state. We will encourage insurers and self-insured entities to develop health care plans that offer these advantages to their subscribers.

We will publish, in addition to the metrics mentioned above with regard to preventable harm, quantitative and clearly understandable data that demonstrates our progress in delivering the kind of health care services outlined above. We will hold ourselves accountable in this fashion, but we will also allow others to hold us accountable. We will jointly advocate, before legislative and regulatory bodies, for government laws and regulations that increase the transparency of the health care delivery system for the public.

Gene later elaborated on our joint vision in a newsletter to his staff, which I also shared with mine. He put what we were doing into the context of the national debate about health care policy, then a major issue facing the country. Here is an excerpt:

"How do we reform healthcare?" That is a big tough question. Politicians can change the way people access care, or how care is financed, but they cannot change how care is delivered and legislators will always find it difficult to create quality.

Only we, the community of practice, can improve quality and change the systems of care in such a way as to improve the experience of care for individuals, improve the health of the nation and end the extortion of much needed funds from the other categories of our collective societal experience. Only we, the good people who provide the care, can create the solutions that end the fragmented, mediocre and unsafe experience of care that is the experience of so many of our citizens.

We control the experience of health care for our patients far more than we might want to admit. Being patient-centered is the hardest task we have because for many of us it means trying very hard to convince patients that they should do what we think is best.

What gets done is usually what we order. If we care about our patients, the first question that must be answered is "What do they really really want?"

The result: After two decades of sending all of their tertiary care and emergency room patients to another Boston hospital, they decided to send half of them to us. This was the largest single shift in market share ever documented in the Boston hospital environment.

But please recall that this did not occur out of an explicit business strategy to garner market share from a competitor. Our goal was to be true to our purpose and to execute a service plan for our patients integrally tied to that purpose. Truly, we would have been content to have done that well, even with no increase in patient volumes. That there was a kindred spirit in the region (i.e., Gene Lindsey) who saw the mutual advantages of a new partnership was serendipitous. Perhaps the lesson, though, is that you make your own luck when you stay true to your purpose.

Interestingly, our initial strategy to emphasize quality, safety, and transparency was initially denigrated by one of the other hospitals in town as "just trying to get a competitive advantage," as if there is something wrong with that— although I have explained to you that the real impetus was much more values-based. Ironically, when asked by a reporter if he would post his hospital's infection rates, the CEO at another institution said to the newspaper, "We'll post our numbers when we are good and ready. But our numbers are better than theirs."

I guess he hadn't read that part of Peter Senge's book.

CHAPTER 6

"You can see things better from here."

DON'T DO THEIR JOB.

John was an experienced adult referee. He was officiating at a high school girls' game in which the coach was continuously and loudly complaining about the calls. After twenty minutes or so, John walked over and silently stood next to the coach, arms crossed, looking out at the game in progress.

"What are you doing?" sputtered the coach. "You're supposed to be out there refereeing."

John calmly replied, "You know, you *can* see things better from here."

At another game, he walked over to a similar coach and said, "I'm so impressed that you are able to both coach the game and referee it. I've always found that I can only do one or the other."

The obvious leadership lesson: If you try to do the other person's job for them by constantly offering unsolicited "helpful advice," you will fail to do your own job well. I have been struck by how many leaders try to do just this, delving into details and otherwise micromanaging their organizations. Unlike John, most people will not let you know that you are doing it. (There is no perceived gain for a subordinate, after all, in criticizing his or her bossy boss.) Accordingly, you will only succeed in undermining their authority and autonomy or getting them upset.

Unfortunately, leaders sometimes resort to this behavior because they feel their board of directors will hold them accountable for the progress of the firm. They forget that focusing on what it takes to create a learning organization is more likely to be successful in meeting corporate strategic objectives.

Edgar Schein comments on this tendency and warns us to avoid "walking in as the boss and expert":

> Many people in senior management positions have the power and the potential to be effective change managers through learning how to help, but their formal position and actual power often lead them into premature fixing. Those at the top of the ladder, in particular, are drawn to the expert ... role, whereas change management really requires the process consultant role.[46]

---

[46] Schein, Edgar H., *Helping, How to Offer, Give, and Receive Help*, Barrett-Kohler Publishers, Inc. San Francisco. 2009. Page 132.

As CEO, I hardly ever made decisions. Instead, I tried to create an environment in which others felt the ability to take charge and to make changes. They also learned to work together in a collaborative and creative—but analytically rigorous—manner to evaluate options and come up with a consensus. More often than not, my job was simply to endorse the work they did and apply hefty doses of positive reinforcement. I also had to train other members of our senior leadership team to do likewise, a task that often took work and persuasion. Let me provide an example.

Meltdown to Turnaround

When I was hired as CEO of Beth Israel Deaconess Medical Center in 2002, the place was in a financial meltdown. A poorly executed merger between New England Deaconess Hospital and Beth Israel Hospital back in 1996 led to poor business planning and the alienation of doctors, nurses, referring physicians from the community, and lay leaders. The hospital had lost $40 million to $70 million per year for five years and had burned through $200 million of its $500 million endowment covering these operating and other one-time losses. The Attorney General of Massachusetts, Tom Reilly, was putting pressure on the board to sell the hospital to a for-profit chain because he had no confidence in its ability to manage the charitable assets represented by its non-profit status.

My first task as CEO was to help our team execute a turn-around. Reilly gave us six months to show progress, demanding a plan, milestones, and periodic reports. This timeline and the reporting requirements were fine with me. I knew it would be clear within six months if we were going to be successful, and we certainly couldn't be successful without a plan, milestones, and periodic reports. The challenge I faced was figuring out how to organize the work required for a turn-around and make sure it would happen in a timely fashion.

The first thing to recognize is that it is the line staff, not the leadership, who will execute a business plan.[47] The best way to ensure their commitment to the plan is to have them develop it, set their own milestones, and report on their results. But the plan they create has to have analytical rigor or it will be based on a bed of sand, of hopeful conjecture rather than solid facts and reasoning.

In our case, a consulting firm, the Hunter Group, had spent months preparing an objective assessment of the hospital's financial and operational condition. That firm had prepared an extensive set of recommendations. Usually such reports are held tightly by senior management, for fear of scaring the staff if the recommendations are made public. Instead, I posted the report on the company website for all to see. I wanted all involved to learn from this independent appraisal of our organization, to evaluate the consultant's recommendations, and to determine which we would accept, which we would reject, and which we would substitute.

---

[47] Here, I refer to a turn-around plan, but the general case also holds with regard to all business plans.

I said to the staff members, "If you don't agree with one of the Hunter Group's recommendations, please explain why, but then you need to give me an alternative that saves as much money. After all, the bottom line is the bottom line, and we have to turn around this deficit." The response was tremendous, following views of the website by thousands of employees and doctors. There were dozens of suggestions, many of which made sense. But there were far more important results from this transparent approach. It created a full understanding of the dimensions of our financial problems, fostered an appreciation for approaching problems openly, and drew strong commitments of support to work together.

Some people who wrote me, like this doctor, referenced the broader health care environment in which our hospital was competing. He understood that we had to restore our reputation in the community:

> Thank you for your direct approach to our problem. We need to rescue this center. It is worth it. Furthermore, we need to restore the public's confidence in our medical center. Many of my patients, friends and outside physicians have shifted to others because of the bad press reports.

Many people made clear a willingness to help. A pulmonologist said, "I have a few small ideas about how to make things better so I am trying to 'think globally and act locally' with my chief. I just wanted to let you know that, although I am busy like everyone else, I am available to serve in whatever capacity might be helpful."

And some colleagues offered a broad, long-term view of the importance of our academic medical center. The chief of oncology wrote, thoughtfully:

> There is a real chance to save [the hospital] even at this late date. Painful cost reductions are clearly inevitable, but the challenge is to do so in a way that preserves the high quality of care that still is present—and which must be our legacy for the future. Should we lose that, even if we save many more dollars, our patients will choose to go elsewhere. Boston is too competitive a marketplace with highly educated consumers. Equally so, we must respond to the physicians in the larger community to enable them to regain confidence in a medical center many of them regarded with awe and affection.

> Although I've not yet had a chance to digest the Hunter report, in scanning it I don't see one important thing in the midst of the numerous "interventions." That is a mandate to continuously measure the quality of service we render using objective medical outcomes and patient experiences. This must not be lost in the drive to lower expenses since it is a barometer of the efficacy of our changes with respect to one of our core missions.

Others felt comfortable about being open with me about their personal fears. A manager in the IT department said: "My team is behind you in the tasks ahead of you. I know that things will not be pleasant at first, but I also know that this is our last chance to get the hospital up to where it needs to be. I am nervous that I may lose my job, as well as is everyone else in the hospital. I hope and pray that I am not one of the unlucky ones and will be able to continue to provide the leadership and technical expertise that I give to the hospital. But my team is behind whatever decisions are needed to turn the hospital around."

Finally, some people just gave me a warm welcome! A secretary in the surgery department noted, "A lot of people are rooting for you and the institution. Welcome and God bless."

These comments and others gave me the confidence that people throughout the organization were fully and positively engaged, as well as informed. It was time to get to work. But how best to organize the work?

Keeping in mind the concept of letting people do their jobs, I chose to create task forces of staff members from middle management (both administrative and clinical) to design the detailed work plan that would form the basis for our turn-around plan. In what may have seemed like an unusual move, I specifically excluded from those task forces the chiefs of service from our various clinical departments (medicine, surgery, radiology, and the like), and I also left off the senior vice presidents of the administrative departments. Not surprisingly, this created some howling, especially from the most senior doctors. Their theme was: "We're in charge here. We need to head up these task forces."

I knew that it would be disastrous to let the chiefs run the process. First of all, while extremely sophisticated and expert in their disciplines, they do not know what is happening on the front-lines of the hospital, which is where change needed to be made. Further—and I say this with great affection and respect—they are not always great listeners. People get ahead in academic medicine by being decisive and opinionated, not by demonstrating great interpersonal skills. If chiefs had been left to chair the committees, they would have intimidated the more junior doctors and administrative staff. Creativity and dissent would have been quashed.

So, I shamelessly prevaricated to the chiefs and said, "Don't worry. The task forces will report up to you and me. We will reserve the right to make any major policy decisions. Then we'll let them do all the grunt work." Of course, I knew that the real work and decisions would be made by the task forces and—given our accelerated timetable for actions—the chiefs wouldn't hear about what had been done until it was mainly over.

Things progressed very well. The turn-around focused on those elements of our business practices that needed fixing. Each task force decided on its priority items, using the Hunter Report as a touchstone to ensure a rigorous review of options and determine how to measure their success. Each initiative adopted specific milestones. People felt empowered and invested in ensuring success. Regular reports were delivered to me, the chiefs, the board, and the Attorney General. I would provide periodic updates to the entire staff by email and in town meetings, celebrating our progress. Within 18 months, we had gone from an operating loss run rate of almost $10 million per month to break-even. The hospital remained profitable for the next seven years of my tenure, and beyond.

Motivating with Expectations:
A Wise Judge Doesn't Use His Power.

It's easy enough to suggest that you sit back and let people do their jobs, but it can be more complex than that. There are times when certain things need to happen and it is your job to define what has to happen but still give people room to do what they need to do.

This was well illustrated during the clean-up of Boston Harbor. The Commonwealth of Massachusetts had been systematically polluting the harbor for decades. In December of 1985, the Massachusetts Water Resources Authority was found guilty of violations of the federal Clean Water Act.[48]

When it came time for the agency to propose a remediation plan and a schedule to build a $3 billion sewage treatment plant and other facilities, the MWRA suggested a schedule that would run about 11 years. The plaintiffs in the case, the U.S. Environmental Protection Agency and the Conservation Law Foundation, demanded much more aggressive milestones. They argued that the Harbor had taken the brunt of sewage pollution for many years and that a fast remediation was needed.

The decision fell to U.S. Federal District Court Judge A. David Mazzone. He had wide leeway in dealing with this case. Federal judges have almost unlimited power and authority in their

---

[48] The MWRA was actually a new agency that took the verdict on behalf of the Commonwealth.

courtrooms. Mazzone understood, though, that the best power is power used sparingly. He also knew how to motivate people.

Without hesitation, Judge Mazzone adopted the plan proposed by the MWRA. Turning to the Authority's chief witness, he said, in essence, "I trust your judgment and believe in your good intentions. I intend to hold you accountable to the schedule you have proposed." His remedial order in May of 1986 codified that decision.

What a wise man. If he had ordered the MWRA to comply with the schedule proposed by the other parties and the agency didn't meet that timetable, the agency could have claimed later that it was because the imposed schedule was unrealistic. Instead, the judge created a situation in which delays could not be explained away, as the timetable was the one proposed by the defendant itself. But note, too, that he presented his decision with an explicit statement of belief in the good intentions and vision of the MWRA to clean the harbor.

The Harbor Cleanup project remained on schedule from that day forward. Years later, Judge Mazzone explained his plan concisely: "I wanted them to take the attitude: 'The Judge gave us this job. The Judge gave us this time. Now, let's do it.' That's the attitude I wanted. And you know what? I did get that."[49]

---

[49] "The Boston Harbor Cleanup Case: Recollections and Reflections from the Mazzone Archives," by Jenni Matz, Urban Harbors Institute, U. Mass, Boston. 2005.

CHAPTER 7

"Just walk it into the goal."

LET SUPERSTARS SHINE.

In the spring of 2005, I had the pleasure of coaching the top under-12 girls team in our town. These kids were spectacular players with great skills and a terrific attitude. They loved to learn, and you could see them improve individually and collectively in every game. They also loved to win. As they arrayed themselves on the field at the start of each game, you could see their confidence. If the opposing team pulled ahead, these girls would not be flustered, they would just play their style of game and take back the lead. The season record was 7–3–0, with our team scoring 26 goals and allowing only 13 against us.

We enrolled in a local Memorial Day tournament that spring and faced a strong opponent in a key game. The Winchester team was very diligent on defense and would pack the goal mouth with their players. No matter how much we tried, we simply could not use our standard attack—going down the outside of the field and crossing the ball to the middle, where it could be deflected past a defender into the goal. Likewise, there was no way to simply take a shot from the outside and hope to penetrate into the goal.

Our star player, Brooke, came off the field for a short substitution break, a bit frustrated that we had not been able to score. I called her over.

"Brooke, you are a terrific dribbler. Next time you go back in, let's forget about passing for a while. Just take the ball and walk it into the net."

She smiled and said, "OK, coach!"

We subbed her back in. She got possession of the ball 25 yards from the goal and dribbled past five defenders and walked the ball into the net. Her teammates gave her high fives and congratulated her on a job well done. We ended up winning the game.

Brooke and teammates

Clearly, on the soccer field and in business, teamwork is important. Coaches and bosses generally have to spend much of their time fostering a team-centered environment and encouraging the best and the brightest to work with others. However, there are times when you should create opportunities for your superstars to shine. If those opportunities are presented in the context of the overall team objectives, you can avoid creating resentment or jealousy on the part of other teammates. As Brooke's story demonstrates, in business, as on the field, you can rely on the drive and skills of your team members. You can use adversity or seemingly intractable problems to create the opportunity for great expectations, and they will often be met.

Ready. Aim. Pull the Trigger.

Let me tell you about another superstar who was given a chance to run. But first, some context:

If you are a patient in one of the nation's academic medical centers, who is watching over you in the middle of the night? Chances are it is a young nurse and an intern, among the least experienced people in the hospital. These folks, though earnest, may not always have the experience and judgment to respond to patient instability.

So imagine, on a regular late night visit to the room, a nurse notices that a patient has developed a fast respiratory rate, a drop in blood pressure, a drop in blood oxygen saturation, or a drop in urine production. She needs to make a decision about whether to call the intern. When the doctor returns the call, s/he needs to decide whether or not to actually come to see the patient, or to just make treatment recommendations over the phone. Then, the intern needs to decide whether to wake up a more senior resident or the attending doctor or to make the decisions around changing the plan of care autonomously. Here's where you should start to worry. There is a reasonable likelihood that this young doctor-in-training does not yet have the experience, knowledge, or sophistication to make a proper judgment about the patient's condition—or (perhaps more scary) to know that s/he doesn't have the ability to make the call.

The next morning, after rounds, the attending or another senior physician arrives and decides that there is a need to change the patient's treatment regime or even move the patient to the ICU because of a severely deteriorated condition. Hours of proper attention have been delayed, and the treatment plan now has to make up for lost time. Or worse, before the attending arrives, the patient suffers cardiac arrest and a "code blue" is called to resuscitate him or her. The point is that when a patient on a medical or surgical unit becomes unstable, early intervention can be very important. Knowing this, the Institute for Healthcare Improvement has recommended that hospitals deploy a rapid response team at the first signs of a patient's decline. But how do you make sure this happens in the middle of the night? Standardizing a response makes a lot of sense when you think about the complex communication systems that exist in most hospitals.

In 2004, a series of events led us to recognize the need to change. First, a journal entitled *Critical Care Medicine* published an article on rapid response teams that caught the attention of our ICU doctors. Next, we had two very serious adverse events in which well-meaning, very involved junior providers did not recognize the speed with which patients might deteriorate. Our folks analyzed those cases and concluded that the care patterns for "acutely decompensating inpatients were complicated, sometimes disorganized, and had multiple single-point failure modes." In short, the inexperienced staff members in charge on the floor were likely to make a series of erroneous decisions when faced with a patient in distress. The most serious problem became evident when we conducted a survey of our house staff (i.e., the interns and residents). We found that they would contact attending physicians for many acute patient events only about 25 percent of the time.

Why wouldn't an intern or resident call the attending physician? Well, part of the mentality of medical training is an overstated belief that *you don't really learn unless you do it yourself.* Young doctors often believe that it will be viewed as a sign of weakness to call for help. Their senior residents reinforce that belief, based on their own experience as junior trainees.

Another factor is the outright fear of calling an attending physician at 2:30 in the morning and getting the following response: "You woke me up for THAT?! What did they teach you in medical school anyway???" (By the way, this reaction is not limited to medicine. I have seen it in many other industries as well.)

All of this suggested an area for major improvement, and one of our superstars, a young doctor named Michael Howell, got to work on the problem. Michael came to BIDMC as a resident and progressed up the ladder to become chief resident in the Department of Medicine, and then a clinical and research fellow in the Harvard Program in Pulmonary & Critical Care Medicine. (He is now an attending physician in the Division of Pulmonary, Critical Care, & Sleep Medicine.)

"From his first days as a trainee, it was clear we had someone special," said Kenneth Sands, MD, senior vice president of health care quality. "His clinical skills were renowned among his fellow residents and there were many anecdotes that circulated about Michael, with his self-deprecating manner, identifying an obscure diagnosis that had eluded more senior clinicians and consultants."

Michael had some intuition about how to solve the problem of decompensating patients based on his literature review of articles from Australia. Early in 2005, he led a six-week pilot program on two medical wards and one surgical ward to test out his version of rapid response teams. Under this program, if a nurse notices that a patient has developed a certain condition, based on a standardized set of criteria ("triggers"), the nurse is required to call the doctor, the senior nurse in charge, and the respiratory therapist—*and they all come to see the patient.* They collaborate on a plan of care for the patient going forward. Regardless of the time of day or night, the intern/resident then calls the attending doctor in charge of the patient to let him/her know that the patient has "triggered."

Under Michael's plan, the standard set of triggers is based on changes in heart rate, blood pressure, oxygen saturation, urine output, an acute change in the patient's conscious state, or a marked nursing concern. The last one, "marked nursing concern," means that if the nurse has any concern whatsoever about the patient, based on observation or instinct, s/he is authorized to call a trigger.

In Michael's experiment, covering 1,845 patient days, there was a significant reduction in deaths. He concluded that "our model was at least as safe as those previously reported."

Michael went to Mark Zeidel, the chief of medicine, and asked permission to expand the experiment and introduce the clinical protocol more widely. It was August of 2005, and Mark had recently arrived from the University of Pittsburgh Medical Center, where he had also served as chief of medicine. He came with a prodigious reputation for making quality and safety improvements in clinical settings, so junior members of the staff often felt intimidated about meeting with him.

Here's how Michael tells the story:

> I am asked to meet with Dr. Zeidel about Triggers. I am terrified. I can't imagine what he's going to think about a fellow running the launch of something like Triggers. The meeting goes something like this:

> MH: "Dr. Zeidel, I'm Mike Howell, one of the pulmonary and critical care [quiet voice, mumble, mumble] fellows. Thanks for the opportunity to take some time to discuss the Triggers program."

> MZ: "Right. Good to meet you. At Pittsburgh, we've had Medical Emergency Teams for a long time. They work really well. They really prevent dithering, and they get the most

experienced person right to the bedside. I'm somewhat ... concerned ... that what you are proposing is too complex, to put it lightly. In Pittsburgh the rescue call brings an intensivist to the bedside. If I understand you right, you are going to have the intern, who then will bring in the resident, who then will to bring in the attending, while the nurse brings in a senior nurse. Isn't that kind of Rube Goldbergesque?"

Since I then had to cardiovert myself out of ventricular tachycardia, this part is a little fuzzy. I talked about the workflow model of my rapid response design concept, compared to the one he had used in Pittsburgh. I felt that his approach was unreliable by its design, and that our goal was to develop high reliability and monitor outcomes carefully.

I also brought a briefing document about our pilot. I think this is what sealed the deal. I had put a lot of thought into it, and the story it told, because *I* had to be convinced that this was the right thing to do. And I was. We reviewed it together and I really remember Dr. Zeidel listening, very carefully, and thinking about the data, and asking a couple of questions.

The room was very quiet for a few seconds, and Dr. Zeidel looked at me, and at Mark Aronson, a senior member of the faculty. "OK," he said. "I am going to let you go forward with this. You've clearly thought a lot about it, you understand the context here— which I don't, yet—and these look like good safety data. But I want to meet every three months and decide—every three months—whether we need to move to a different model."

I now had enough rope to hang myself with. And the Triggers Program was born.

Looking back, I realize what a pivotal moment of leadership this was— Dr. Zeidel having worked at the best Medical Emergency Team hospital in the country (Pittsburgh), which had a very (very!) different approach, and to come here and listen, evaluate, and be convinced that it was reasonable to try a totally different model ... while setting up some safety and monitoring bounds. I'm not sure I would have been able to do the same, but I'm glad he could.

Well, it turned out that Howell's program was incredibly effective. Over the course of the first year, the hospital observed significant reductions in "code blue" cardiac arrest events and a significant reduction (a 47% decrease) in relative risk of non-ICU death for our patients. Residents now needed to practice emergency resuscitation mainly in the simulation center because so few actual patients needed it. What a lovely problem to have. We also learned a lot about teamwork, communication, and systems of care as a result of closely reviewing our responses to called triggers.

But here's the clincher. Dr. Zeidel now proudly and widely tells the story of how a young fellow had the nerve to tell a chief of medicine that his boss had no substantive support for his opinion and that it was important to conduct a scientifically based experiment to test the efficacy of a new clinical protocol. The leadership displayed by Dr. Zeidel in this respect is precisely of the type I have been discussing in this book. As coach, Mark let his superstar excel, to the benefit of the entire organization. He has the modesty to admit to the world that, absent Michael's calm forcefulness, he would have stood in the way of significant progress. He tells us all that he learned a lesson from this story that he now applies widely.

In 2007, the hospital also gave its highest award to Michael Howell for his work in this arena, but I think that the comments his chief of service continues to make worldwide mean more to him than any award we could give.

Framing the Success of Superstars as Part of the Team's Success

The key in allowing a superstar to take off without upsetting the overall concept of working together as a team is in how you communicate with the staff about what these superstars are doing. Handled the right way, you can hold up those who have done well in a way that inspires rather than demoralizes others.

You have several options as leader with regard to the communication mechanisms you use to present these successes so they are viewed in the context of the team's overall objectives. Award ceremonies, for instance, can be useful in this regard. Company-wide emails are another option. I found that the new tools of social media were also very helpful. Over my years running BIDMC, I maintained an active and widely-read blog, called *Running a Hospital*. I often used the blog to "brag" about the particular accomplishments of high-achieving individuals and groups within the hospital. People loved to read those stories about themselves and would forward the link to dozens of friends, families, and co-workers. I think it meant a lot to them, too, that the blog was on the Internet for the entire world to see, which reinforced my initial inclination to use this medium.

The blog posts also often gave the superstar a chance to build teamwork by complimenting others who had made a contribution to his or her success. In one blog post, for example, I praised two of our pancreatic surgeons, Mark Callery and Charles Vollmer, for outstanding clinical out-comes. Then I quoted Dr. Vollmer's note to the medical staff:

> This week Mark and I celebrated a significant milestone with the performance of our 600th major pancreatic resection over the last eight years together here at BIDMC. This has come with an overall perioperative mortality rate of 1.3%, as well as other benchmark quality outcomes.
>
> As you can tell from the size of the address string above, this has not come solely at our hands, but rather has been achieved by a collaborative effort among some of the world's finest doctors in the field of pancreas care. We are indebted to your skill, acumen, foresight and friendship. With continued dedication and hard work, we look forward to sharing further accomplishments with you.

Don't Just Exploit Superstars, Create Them

Here's a little secret I have never disclosed. I also used the blog to "create" superstars. People in all kinds of positions in the hospital—who might never have viewed themselves as special contributors—discovered that they were, in fact, quite special in their accomplishments.

Gloria Martinez, one of the transporters at our hospital, was one example. Her job was to push patients through the hospital in wheelchairs and beds, but also to deliver specimens from the GI procedure rooms to the pathology laboratory. One day, she noticed flaws in that delivery process leading to misplaced samples. Understanding the clinical consequences of losing valuable human tissues, she brought the problem to the attention of her supervisor. As a result, the entire process by which specimens were transported was redesigned, eliminating a potentially disastrous problem. Our Board of Directors recognized Gloria for this call-out, which I then wrote about on my blog so that more people would see the story.[50]

I wrote again about her reporting when she accepted an award in front of the hospital's Board of Directors:

[50] http://runningahospital.blogspot.com/2008/12/caller-outer-award-of-month.html

When Gloria Martinez, one of our transporters, won our first caller-outer-of-the-month award, she first graciously accepted the award on behalf of herself and the other transporters. Then, with no coaching or prompting whatsoever, she said that she and her colleagues viewed their job as "trying to provide the kind of care we would want members of our own family to receive."

I know I do not violate confidences when I tell you that this simple statement from Gloria left tears in the eyes of our Board members. That a person who pushes beds and wheelchairs and delivers specimens—who in another institution might be anonymous and ignored—could simply and elegantly express the community purpose of our hospital was very moving.51

I know, from the traffic report I received on that blog post, that it was circulated far and wide throughout the hospital, not just among Gloria's own group, but to hundreds of other employees. That she (a native Spanish-speaker, no less) took it upon herself to call out a problem that was of importance to the care of our patients was setting an example throughout the organization.

Other institutions use their own versions of caller-outer awards to recognize star behavior in their midst. Johns Hopkins Medicine, for example, has a Good Catch Award. As noted in a 2010 paper presented to the Maryland Patient Safety Center:

---

51 http://runningahospital.blogspot.com/2010/04/non-zero-sum.html

The Good Catch Award creates positive incentives for providers and staff to report patient safety events. At the institutional level, the Good Catch Award encourages individuals to identify and report adverse events, near misses, or other medical errors. The program rewards individuals who contribute and has been received positively by many providers and staff. The pilot phase of this program focused on identifying defects in the perioperative environment and devising a partial solution. The current phase of the Good Catch Award program shifts its focus to sustainability and strategies to maintain the implemented systems changes that resulted from the 13 Good Catch Awards given in the past two and a half years. This includes an educational component for providers, one of the original steps in the Good Catch Award process, to ensure better dissemination of information and implementation of systems improvements throughout the ACCM department. The program is ongoing in its effort to identify defects, formulate solutions, and recognize those who actively work to create a safer environment.[52]

We can summarize this chapter by saying the following: While democracy is great and important, and while it is essential to be respectful of each person's contribution to the organization, not all team members are created equal. When there are superstars in your group, give them a chance to shine, consistent with the organization's strategy. Explain their

---

[52] "The Good Catch Award: Sustaining Solutions with Practice-Based Learning and Improvement," MPSC 2010 Annual Conference, http://www.marylandpatientsafety.org/html/education/solutions/201 0/documents/culture/The_Good_Catch.pdf

accomplishments as being part of the team effort. And be alert to the fact that not all superstars put themselves forward as such: You might need to do a little "marketing" to let the world know that you have a top draft choice in your midst.

CHAPTER 8

"We'll design the warm-up, Coach."

GET OUT OF THEIR WAY.

It was spring, and the 18-year-old high school seniors were playing their last semester of soccer. Given all their other activities and years of experience playing together, there were no weekly practices. We met only on Sunday afternoons at the game field. This was a town team in a regional league, but the league standings didn't matter, as there would be no championship round. The girls had all been accepted into college and were coasting through their last weeks of high school.

We arrived at the game field a half-hour before the start of the game, and I launched into my coaching role, suggesting that they warm up, something that by this time in their soccer careers they knew how to do.

Had they been younger, I would have guided them. With junior teams, I watch the players go through the early drills, attuned to their psychological readiness for the game. If there's lethargy, for example, I might introduce a quick game of keep-away to prime the competitive juices. As the girls get older, however, I let them use more of their own discretion in the warm-up, which provides a good chance for team-building. Still, I keep an eye on things to make sure they are covering the basics. There is a parallel in executive leadership. In the early stages of corporate team building, you need to help establish the rules of behavior. Over time, people in the company internalize them, and you are left in more of a maintenance and reminder mode.

On that spring day, those 18-year-olds went to an extreme. They sat on the grass in a circle, talking, while nudging a soccer ball with their feet from one player to another. My coaching instincts and common sense told me they should be doing something a bit more productive and physically demanding. I gently suggested they get up and do some passing.

They wanted none of it.

"We'll design the warm-up, coach," was the response.

I was astute enough to get busy doing something else. After all, these were adults who understood the context of their behavior and the consequences of being unprepared for the game. Beyond that, I figured that they were of such an age that self-motivation would rule, not the comments of a coach they only saw once a week. But I have to admit that part of me was thinking, "So you think you're so smart. Wait till you get out on the field and get smashed."

The game began and ended. All the girls were smiling as they walked to their cars. We had won by a huge margin against a very good team. In fact, we dominated the entire game. Our team's communication, passing, and ball control during the game was sharp and effective. It showed that sometimes you just have to chill out and let people enjoy each other's company. Not every moment can or should contain strategically or tactically important activities. Some moments are for socialization. This lubricant helps people through the tough times.

On that day, in this game, the socialization that had gone on for years prior proved invaluable. The girls didn't need a more extensive warm up because they knew each other and they knew their strategy, how they would play "their" game.

These girls were headed in different directions after they graduated, so maybe they were relaxed about the game, too. It mattered less than previous games or tournaments, for example. Nonetheless, there was a good lesson here. In more tumultuous times and stressful situations, in an organization that is going to face ups and downs, having a strong social bond can make the difference between surviving a disaster or not.

So, in your company, it will matter much more than on that spring day on a soccer field. You will do well to find ways to bring people together. It may seem frivolous, but it can make a

significant difference, as we discovered at Beth Israel
Deaconess Medical Center.

Following a Merger Disaster: Building Relationships

When I arrived at BIDMC in 2002, the place was in crisis, and
we had to spend the better part of a year implementing a
difficult turn-around plan. After that year, it was clear that we
had staunched the bleeding. This breakthrough meant we
would survive. The next question was whether we could do
more than that: Could we thrive? We faced many new types of
challenges, the kind that would take an engaged, positive,
flexible, nimble, and creative staff—a staff that could not only
work in teams but also do so in a way that would be mutually
supportive and consistent with deeply held values of caring.

To put it mildly, that was not exactly what we had. BIDMC
came out of the 1996 merger of Beth Israel Hospital and the
New England Deaconess Hospital, each of which had its own
distinct culture and a sense of family. Leadership decisions
made after the merger had failed to bring the two together.
Although merged in name, the staff was still largely divided
according to the hospital for which employees had originally
worked. "Oh, they're BI people," would say the Deaconess
folks. "Oh, they're Deaconess people," would say the BI
people. Nobody was saying that they were "BIDMC" people.
There was no clear sense of a new joint culture, much less the
feelings of support and camaraderie that could be characterized as a family.

It was around this time, in 2003, that the general counsel of
BIDMC, Patricia McGovern, suggested to me that we invite a

group of 15 to 20 mid-level managers to an off-site location for conversation, group games (like "two truths and a lie" and Trivial Pursuit), dinner, and wine to get to know one another.

Pat, who had served in the State Senate, truly understands the importance of camaraderie. The political battles in the Legislature could be quite fierce, but the relationships among the senators were collegial because they had come to know one another personally. It wasn't rare to make impassioned speeches in the well of the State House in opposition to a colleague and then right afterwards go out for a beer together.

For us, the game gatherings, of which there were several, were a great opportunity for people to open up and relate in new ways.

"I have been sending you emails for five years, but I never met you," was one typical reaction. "You go hang-gliding!" said another. "You have how many children?!" would be another.

People got to know one another as individuals and members of their community, separate from their work responsibilities. They discovered that they enjoyed each other's company. Later, back in the office, they remembered and treated one another with much less of a bureaucratic attitude. They became more helpful, considerate, and empathic towards their colleagues.

The dinner sessions also gave our managers a chance to see their CEO in a different context, to learn that my hopes and aspirations were remarkably congruent to their own. It gave me a chance to reinforce the leadership philosophy that you have seen throughout this book. I was able to make clear that I trusted them and was there to support them. They, in turn, developed more trust in me.

Pat and I held dozens of dinners over the course of three years, with a different group each time, engaging hundreds of mid-level managers. These sessions contributed greatly to a sense of camaraderie in our hospital and led to working relationships that were productive, trusting, mutually respectful and, indeed, affectionate. The sense of personal and professional interdependence among the various departments in the hospital was evident. The nurse managers and finance people now knew the heads of the transport service, the housekeepers, and the food service workers. It started to feel like a family again.

This camaraderie was useful when we were engaged in the Lean process improvement efforts discussed in Chapter 3, which were dependent on managerial support for interdivisional task forces. An inherent part of the Lean process improvement philosophy is that front-line workers are encouraged, empowered, and expected to call out problems in the work environment to their supervisors. This philosophy, in turn, requires supervisors to be receptive to those call-outs. It only works if they respond politely, pleasantly, and effectively.

But the sense of interdependence turned out to be crucial when the organization faced a financial meltdown that could have disrupted the entire system and our ability to carry out our mission.

Testing Our Sense of Purpose

In the spring of 2009, halfway through the fiscal year, we found that the nationwide recession and other factors had thrown our hospital finances into a tizzy. Instead of heading toward a year-end surplus of $20 million, which we had projected when we wrote our budget at the start of the fiscal year, we were looking at a loss of that amount—a swing of $40 million in just six months. It was clear that a loss of that magnitude would have an impact for years to come. The income from operations is virtually the only source of funding for a hospital's capital investment. Even during good years, a hospital is fortunate if it can earn a three percent margin, barely enough to cover the depreciation of plant and equipment. Major losses mean having to put off important upgrades or replacing medical equipment. Infrastructure maintenance and replacement are likewise deferred, affecting the functioning and appearance of buildings and services. Even strategic investments in the hospital and with affiliated physician groups and community hospitals are delayed, putting the hospital at a competitive disadvantage.

In our case, the impact would have been more than the tangible inability to invest and upgrade. The hospital had only had a few years of surpluses following a half a decade of post-merger multi-million dollar losses. To dip back down so far into the red would have been morally devastating to our staff and doctors. It also would have been a sign to our external constituents, particularly major donors, that we were weak, unstable, and perhaps unworthy of their future support.

The clock was ticking. Our run rate was negative $400,000 per week on an annualized basis. But since we had only six months to turn around the finances to break even, we needed to garner savings of twice that amount per week to break even by the end of the fiscal year. My senior advisers told me that we would have to lay off several hundred staff members to meet the target. They advised that we should immediately begin to contact vice presidents to construct a layoff list, make the decisions, and send out pink slips. I disagreed.

I felt that we had a tightly knit community in the hospital that would stand together and agree to make sacrifices in order to save the jobs of their fellow workers. I believed that if I asked the question the right way, framing the issue in terms of mutually held values, the staff would "design their own warm-up," solving the financial problem more quickly and effectively and humanely than a centralized approach based on layoffs. I felt that way because of the time I had spent with hundreds of our managers, who now knew each other as well. I had seen their sense of mutual purpose and collaboration grow, not only during Pat's dinners, but, as noted above, in many of the Lean improvement events, trainings, and the like.

Based on that belief, I sent the following note to the staff:

> At stressful times like this, there is a natural tendency to feel fear. Most of us have families to support or other obligations that go beyond the basics of food, clothing, and shelter. We try our best to plan our lives and live carefully and frugally, saving for future contingencies. Then, an earthquake-like phenomenon occurs, a massive disruption in our economic system that shakes the very foundations of decisions about

consumption, savings, and personal security. Add to this a follow-on tremor by telling you that the hospital has been affected by the broad economic issues and that we will have to make tough decisions that will affect you personally.

I know that this is very distressing. In my view, we have two ways to respond. We can retreat into isolation from one another. That path leads to resentment, distrust, and a slow degradation of the work environment and of the sense of mission of our hospital. Or, we can look within and find that the values which have guided our care of patients and families are also the same values that apply to our care for one another. In the words of Lois, a manager in our Department of Medicine, "I think we will learn much from the process. I even dare to believe that we will become a community of healing for one another, just as we are for our patients."

This note was followed by the first of several "town meetings" to solicit ideas from the staff for cutting expenses to avoid layoffs. My intention was to get them to throw ideas on the table, all requiring a bit of sacrifice from all to save a few. We might defer raises, or reduce vacation time or 401(k) matching contributions, for example. I also made clear that we had little time to decide. Decisive action was called for, and it would entail sacrifices for all.

The town meeting: Why are these people smiling?

As I was running the first town meeting, however, another thought occurred to me. Without asking anybody, I decided to pose a challenge to the assembled group. Even years later, I remain a bit surprised at my audacity, but I somehow knew at the time that we had a chance to create a huge learning opportunity for the entire organization. It could cement, in ways never considered, the set of values that underlay everything our hospital stood for. It was a way to banish forever any residual distinctions between "BI people" and "Deaconess people." It was a way to affirm our respect for one another.

Consequently, I added another item to the agenda of the first town meeting and all subsequent ones. I said that I wanted to run an idea by the staff and get their reaction to it. I explained that I wanted to protect the lower wage earners, the transporters, the housekeepers, the food service staff—those who have more contact with patients than anyone else.

My feeling was, as I told the crowd, that many of these workers were recent immigrants working hard to support families both here and in their home countries, and I didn't want to put an additional burden on them. So I proposed that they should be exempt from all of the potential cutbacks and wage freezes we were discussing.

I explained that protecting those workers would mean the rest of us would have to make bigger sacrifices. With only slight trepidation, I asked how they would feel about doing that. I expected that they would agree, but I did not expect what happened next.

The auditorium erupted in applause. It was an overwhelming outpouring of community spirit. It did, indeed, reinforce our underlying values as I had hoped. Others felt the same way. Here's one example, from Brenda, a nurse in our neonatal intensive care unit:

> Paul,
>
> I attended today's 4pm town meeting and about halfway through the meeting, I found myself on the verge of tears. Not just because of how worried I am, and not because of how sad the situation makes me, but because of how overwhelmingly proud I feel to be a part of the BIDMC community.
>
> I have worked in the NICU since November 2007, so I am pretty new to the hospital. I have worked in several different

hospitals and I have never witnessed what I witnessed today. First you began by telling us how hard you were trying to avoid layoffs. Any CEO could say that. But what impressed me was the deeply human way you explained how difficult this process is. The fact that you are considering that many employees' spouses have already lost jobs, and that you know employees who lose jobs will have a very hard time finding new ones showed such compassion and respect that I was stunned. However, your request that we try to minimize the effect any cuts will have on the lowest-paid employees was what brought me to tears—that and the loud applause you received after making that request.

I know the next few months will be extremely difficult for all of us. But it is so comforting to know that the people I work with are not just sitting back and letting things happen. After this afternoon's meeting, we had our own "post-town meeting meeting" to review what you had said, and to toss around suggestions. I know those little meetings are happening all over the medical center. I have never been prouder of the people I work with and the hospital I work for.

I followed up the town meetings by asking people for their ideas, and I got hundreds of emails. I also immediately set up a chat room to encourage people to comment on one another's suggestions. Social media makes this kind of communication powerful, especially in an organization that runs 24 hours a day, with multiple shifts. Why? Because of its inherent asynchronicity. You don't have to read another person's comment when it is posted. You can go to the chat room at your leisure, and multiple times, catching up on submissions and comments, and offering your own whenever you like. I received about 2,700 suggestions and comments in the form of direct emails, Facebook messages, and messages in the chat room. For context, we had at the time about 6,400 full-time equivalent employees and about 800 doctors.

After the first round of comments, I sent a message outlining ideas that I was thinking of adopting. Employees responded with another 800 messages and chat room suggestions. A third and final message with a detailed budget plan drew about 100 comments.[53]

The consensus was that the staff members did not want anyone to get laid off and were willing to give up pay and benefits to help make sure that was possible. Here are some examples of comments I received:

Brian from the Finance Department said:

> Obviously, I want to keep this job. I'm sure I echo most people's thoughts when I say that no one wants anyone else to be laid off, and we are all willing to do whatever is necessary to make sure that as few as possible actually lose their jobs.
>
> I think the ideas on taking pay cuts, or maybe working one day a week less, can work. I stand behind whatever decisions you and the Senior Management team make. Thank you for your candor, and please keep us all informed!

Catherine, a nurse, said:

---

[53] http://runningahospital.blogspot.com/2009/04/paul-solman-on-pbs-tells-bidmc-story.html

I would be more than happy to forgo a pay raise and reduce my earned time if that would mean another person in the hospital could keep their job. I think this is a great idea and I hope my colleagues feel the same.

And Bernice, an MRI technician, agreed:

I would rather take the loss of my yearly raise than see a fellow employee laid off.

Step By Step

Let's summarize the key aspects of this story, as it contains leadership lessons applicable to other situations. Yes, we have let the players "design their own warm-up," but I had to create a context and format within which that design could meet the strategic needs of the organization. The bottom line, after all, was the bottom line. We had to get to break-even, and quickly. What were those steps?

First, before talking with the staff as a whole, I asked the senior leadership, all the vice presidents, to voluntarily take a five percent pay cut and give up their next year's pay increase. I told them that I would set the example by agreeing to the same terms but with a ten percent base salary deduction. Every single person rapidly and willingly agreed to this.

Knowing what I was going to ask of the staff, I felt that this move was essential. I didn't want anyone on the staff to feel like a sap, giving up their pay and benefits while those of us in the C-suite kept ours. I also needed to anchor the forthcoming discussion about pay and benefit decreases by publicizing the five percent pay cut figure. I figured that this amount, more or less, was what would be required from everyone else. Having heard the number would make it more acceptable to the staff.

The key next step was to be utterly transparent with staff about the nature of the financial problems. Knowing that you can't engage in collaborative problem solving unless there is a common base of knowledge and information, I asked my CFO to prepare just a few slides that we could use at the start of our town meetings to explain the situation in simple declarative sentences (i.e., what's going on and why there is a problem). I also carefully crafted my emails on the topic. I needed to write in such a way that someone who was not spending all their time in the finance office could still read and understand what I was saying. I needed to be sure that a nurse or respiratory therapist or doctor who was busy doing something else—who would only spend about three minutes reading my email—would get the major points.

Here are some excerpts from the first email:

> As you can see from general trends in the economy and by watching the actions of other hospitals, the situation has gotten worse. For BIDMC, our hoped-for 2% FY09 operating margin (about $18 million) has disappeared. The state has reduced Medicaid payments by over $7 million, our major insurer is paying us less than we had hoped, and research funding has also fallen short by several million dollars. In addition, patient volumes are substantially lower than budgeted as people in the community defer or forego medical visits and treatments.

Right now, at best, we can break even for the year if patient volumes return to budgeted levels. However, if they stay at current levels, we will face an operating loss of up to $20 million. This is the contingency for which we must prepare, or else we will have insufficient funds to invest in the buildings, plant, and equipment needed.

Part of the solution to this problem will be to lay off people. I'm not sure how many yet, and I am hoping you can help me figure out how to minimize the number by using more creative and less disruptive ways to solve the problem. I am going to hold some town meetings in the next several days to get your thoughts about alternative concepts. I will lay out some ideas here, so you can be thinking about them. You can write back now, or you can tell me in person later. Perhaps you will want to discuss them with your colleagues. Perhaps you have better ideas to suggest. We'll soon set up an electronic chat room, too, to permit people to share their thoughts more broadly with the community.

Our focus has to be on reduction of personnel costs, our major operating expense. Here are some ideas to start the discussion: Eliminate the 3% pay raise for people who would ordinarily receive it starting April 1. (To compensate, in the future, new raises could start with the people who have anniversary dates of April 1 and after.) Reduce future earned time accruals by one or two days per year. Forfeit one or two days of past accruals of earned time. Permit certain floors or units to avoid layoffs by voluntarily taking pay cuts equivalent to the dollars that would be saved by the layoffs in that floor or unit. Ask people to take furloughs, unpaid leaves of absence for several days.

But the bottom line is the bottom line. If you don't like these
ideas, please help us come up with others.

As indicated above, the next step was to provide convenient
forums for people to provide suggestions. We used the town
halls, but also created the aforementioned chat room. From
the start, the chat room was designed to be completely open
and totally anonymous (leading to some developments I cover
in the next section). Plus, of course, staff had access to me in
the hallways, and by email, and on Facebook. [54]

The next element was to be respectful of people's input. I
made it very clear that I would listen to what people said,
addressing some of the common themes, explaining why I
tended to agree or disagree. But I also made clear that I had
not made up my mind, and I asked for further comments and
suggestions. Here are some excerpts from that email:

> It has been a very busy couple of weeks, with thousands of
> you attending town meetings and sending suggestions to me
> personally or on our chat page. As promised, here's my
> analysis of the options we have considered and suggestions
> for going forward. This is going to be a long message, so grab
> a cup of coffee while you read it. I apologize if I don't address
> each and every idea that has been suggested, but I am pretty

---

[54] I had accumulated well over 1,000 staff as "friends" on Facebook
during the previous three years, inviting employees to join me during
my welcoming remarks at the weekly new employee orientation. This
became the favorite mode of communication between staff members
in their 20s and me: It turned out that they weren't using email as much
as the older generation of staff.

sure I will cover the major ones. At the end of this e-mail, I will tell you how you can best provide input into the next stage of this process.

First, though, an important summary. Your participation in this process and your advice to me have succeeded in accomplishing two very important things: First, we have reduced the number of necessary layoffs dramatically, from over 600 to about 150. This is a major victory and will mean a lot to more than 450 families who would otherwise lose their income from BIDMC. Second, we will do this at the same time we provide earnings protection to our 900 lowest wage workers. As you will see, this does come at a higher cost to the rest of us, but you have all made clear to me that this is consistent with our community's values and expectations. Thank you in advance for your generosity of spirit.

And after listing my initial thoughts, I concluded:

Now, for your reactions to this list of more concrete options: We have set up a new chat room called Budget Forum 2. Please offer your thoughts there until 5 p.m. on Thursday, March 19. (The original Budget Brainstorm chat room will remain up for observation, but it will no longer be possible to post comments there.) ... And, of course, feel free to write me directly as well by return e-mail.

I will issue another e-mail within a week with my final decisions and more details on these matters.

The final step was to explain the logic of my decisions, making clear that I listened to what people had said and respected it. I also did my best to put the decisions in terms of the underlying value structure of our hospital. In my last budget message of the sequence, I said:

I believe that we work in this particular hospital because we have come to trust the BIDMC family to care for one another. My decisions below are guided by this premise. Some of you will disagree with aspects of what I have decided, or the rationale for them. I have read and heard those views in your comments on the chat room and in personal emails. I promise you that I have seriously considered those views, and that I respect them, but there comes a time when I need to balance competing concerns and make a decision that will not be popular with all. Please trust and understand that I don't take on this role with a belief that my views matter more than any of yours, but because it is sometimes my job to try to consolidate and reflect back the underlying ethical and moral judgments that you have expressed to me. I believe that this is one of those times, and that we as a hospital will be judged by the broader community for how we handle these issues.

So, my decisions below are guided by some social principles as well as business principles. As noted from the outset, I will do what I can to protect the lowest wage earners among us. Even, above that income level, I will tend to ask proportionally greater sacrifices from those higher up in the income stream than those below. I do not do this because I believe people earning in the mid-range or even the high range have fewer financial obligations than the others. I know there are people earning $70,000 or even over $100,000 with very tight budgets and lots of financial commitments. But, as a general matter, people who have been earning more for years do have more options and assets than those who have earned less. I feel an obligation, therefore, to skew our budget relief plan in a manner that asks more of those higher up the wage scale.

Too Much Freedom of Expression?

The risk of opening up the conversation, even with the best of intentions, is that not everyone will participate in a positive manner. You will likely get nasty, unproductive, and mean remarks when you set up a chat room that allows anonymous comments. This started to occur at BIDMC. A small number of commenters were very negative and sometimes rude.

When others began reading the negative comments, some were offended and asked me to take down the chat room. For example, one person said, "Take this brainstorming session down. I am embarrassed to say I work with these people!!" Others asked me to delete the nasty comments.

I refused to do either. Unfortunately, people who comment anonymously sometimes say things that are ill-conceived or mean, but the forum was still useful and important to those who were taking it seriously. To take it down, to dismantle that attempt at openness, would have been to let those who misbehave steal an opportunity from those of us who wanted to participate.

Instead, I started to post a reply after each nasty comment suggesting to the author that he or she was engaged in bad behavior, was insulting their fellow workers, or was otherwise undermining the spirit of openness and collaboration that we sought to foster.

Interestingly, staff members, too, started to post their own comments encouraging better behavior. Here's a sample:

> Before you scoff at an idea presented, think about how fortunate we are to have this forum in which to 'vent' and to present ideas. Most companies just make decisions regarding cutbacks and notify their employees once the decisions are made. We are being given a unique opportunity here to be part of the conversation and ultimately the solution. Be mature and show some respect to everyone that at least comes to the table with something.

The percentage of nasty comments diminished dramatically and quickly. We had proven that people of good intent could overcome the naysayers. We had reinforced that a mode of behavior encouraging openness and collaboration could be more powerful than a culture of negativism.

The Payoff

The end result of this entire process was that we were able to balance the budget with hardly any layoffs. And much to our amazement, we achieved national renown for our hospital. Readers emailed a *Boston Globe* story by Kevin Cullen detailing the events to over 14,000 other people around the world.[55] The story was also posted on the Yahoo home page for an entire day, viewed there by hundreds of thousands of people.

---

[55] Kevin Cullen, "A head with a heart," *Boston Globe*, March 12, 2009. http://www.boston.com/news/local/massachusetts/articles/2009/03/12/a_head_with_a_heart/

ABC news, NBC news,[56] and PBS all came to do feature stories, seen by millions of viewers. The pride among our staff was palpable. Patients, too, felt a part of the story and helped spread the word. Here's a note from Bob, who had had cardiac surgery at our hospital:

> I just watched the NBC clip about the employees of BI. I must tell you how much I appreciated the care that I received from all of the folks who attended to me while I was recovering from my surgery. This is most true of the 'low-level' employees. The folks who helped me wash, brought me my meals and took me for my x-rays were all professional and courteous. For this reason alone, I am so glad to hear of the efforts all of the BIDMC employees to ensure that everyone can keep their jobs.

About a year and a half later, we were able to restore the salary and benefits to our staff, and even pay a small bonus when our business improved.

Jerry wrote a typical response:

> I'm sure you were inundated with thank you emails for this bonus, but I felt the need to add mine to the list. I also wanted to mention that when I told my wife about this she said, "What a wonderful place to work. That would have never happened at my company."

---

[56] http://runningahospital.blogspot.com/2009/04/peter-alexander-tells-bidmcs-and.html

I'm sure the five hundred dollars will come in handy, but the fact that our leadership even thought of this is what makes BIDMC such a great place to work. We came together when times were tough, and now we are sharing the wealth as finances improve. To me this sounds more like a family than a workplace.

And all because I had let them "design the warm up," trusting in their wisdom to do what was best for the team.

Get Over Your Fear of Losing Control

Why is it that more leaders do not engage in this kind of public crowd-sourcing of ideas and suggestions from their staff when the organization faces an important challenge? Fear of losing control. Let me give you two examples.

Around the time BIDMC was going through this crisis, I was talking with the president of a major university that was facing similar financial pressures because of the downturn in the US economy. I suggested that it might be helpful to solicit ideas from all of the faculty and administrative staff, as well as students, as to how to deal with the problem—and to do so in an open forum that would permit people to comment on one another's suggestions. I pointed out that those who were social media literate would be especially likely to participate and provide real value to the administrative leadership. The reaction from this president: "Participation is one thing, pandemonium is another."

And, back at BIDMC, after we had succeeded in this approach—avoiding layoffs, raising morale, and creating a greater sense of community—I was talking with one of my board members. This person, who was one of the leaders of a major financial institution, said, "I never would have had the nerve to do what you did." I replied, "Why does it take any nerve? You are bound to get some good ideas. Also, having asked people for their suggestions, they are much more likely to accept the measures that you ultimately decide to implement." The reply: "I would fear losing control."

Leaders who believe they have control over the dozens or hundreds or thousands of people in their division, department, or corporation are deceiving themselves. Sure, leaders can determine salaries and promotions and even strategic priorities, but they do not control the people with whom they work. Each one of those people is an individual, guided by his or her own values, intuition, fears, and hopes. The leader's success is measured by how well he or she has properly created an environment in which each person can employ his or her intellect, creativity, and energy in support of the purpose of the organization and feel appreciated for having done so. A crisis is too valuable an opportunity to waste in crystallizing that kind of outcome.

The BIDMC staff never had a doubt during this episode that I was still the CEO, with all the authority and responsibility inherent in that position. But there was also never a doubt that I truly cared about each person's point of view and that I trusted each one to be a valuable member of our team, guided by the greater good in support of our purpose—and of each other. There was never a stronger sense of the "BIDMC family" than at this moment, with dividends extending beyond our staff, inuring to our patients and the broader community.

CHAPTER 9

"I'm sorry."

WHAT HAPPENS WHEN YOU REALLY LET DOWN YOUR TEAM?

My buddy Dave has been a coach for many years, and his philosophy and approach to teaching the girls is very similar to mine, one highly respectful to them as individuals. He doesn't yell at the players. He runs his practices and games in a manner that empowers individual creativity and group learning. He is empathic, kind, and considerate. We consider him to be one of the best coaches in the league and often assign him to lead our premier team. Loving to be with the children and teach them, he, like me, has continued to coach teams well after his own daughter outgrew the program.

But even the best of coaches can have an off moment. Dave's came while his team played on a beautiful field surrounded by a lovely wooded area. As he explains:

> I was coaching the top under-14 girls team in a hotly con-
> tested match against Dedham. The Dedham kids historically

are tough and often chippy, and this match was no different. The Newton girls were getting pretty frustrated with the verbal "abuse" they were taking. (You've heard it, in only the way that 13- and 14-year-old girls can dish it.)

The game was tied, 1-1, early in the second half. My star striker, Michele, was clearly fouled and pulled down in the 18-yard box from behind by a Dedham defender. There was no call by the referee. I was livid and turned and tossed my clipboard into the woods. All the players on the bench, as well as the rather large clot of fans on the far touchline, saw me do it.

Two seconds later, I'm thinking, "What are you doing?!"

Regardless, the game continued and we ended up scoring twice late in the second half to win.

At this point, having won the game, Dave could have ignored his own outburst and moved onto the celebration. He felt, however, that would not have been in the best interest of his team.

After the match, I told the girls they needed to stay for 5 minutes to talk. I took them over to the baseball backstop, away from the parents and other fans, and sat them down. I apologized to them for embarrassing them by my outburst and told them that there is no place in sports, let alone our team, for that kind of behavior. I asked them to understand that while I try very hard to set a good example around sporting behavior, not everyone is perfect. And I asked them to forgive me, with my promise that I would make sure that anything like that never, ever happened again.

One of the girls raised her hand, and I asked her what she wanted to say. In a nutshell, she said, "Coach D, it's no big deal. We see so much worse behavior out of the other teams we play every week, by players, coaches and fans. We love that you are so against that kind of stuff. It makes us feel special that you care so much about how other people see us and think about us. We mess up so much, it's amazing you don't yell at us!"

There was lots of nodding and smiles, followed by one of the best-feeling group hugs I've ever experienced!

Dave and team

Dave understood that, as a leader, you are not just another person working in the organization. The nature of your position means that you are expected to personify the values of the company. When you stray from those values, you undermine the cultural ethic that embodies the purpose of the firm, and you therefore undermine the very effectiveness of the organization. Your action demoralizes the people in the firm. I use that term "demoralizes" as having two meanings: (1) making people feel badly about their work environment and (2) lowering the standard of behavior for others. So, beyond any need the leader might have for personal redemption, he or she needs to act promptly and effectively to acknowledge, apologize, and remediate his or her errors for the good of the organization. Understanding these points, we can now turn to the lessons.

The first lesson is that a good leader offers candid and early admission of errors to his or her team. It is important to indicate your acknowledgment of the mistake while it is still fresh, to avoid any perception that you are attempting to recharacterize it or redefine its importance. Delay of apology risks causing resentment among those who have been aggrieved.

The second lesson is that if you habitually help members of your team see that their errors and omissions are moments for learning rather than opportunities to cast blame, then you as an individual are also more likely to allow yourself to likewise learn from your own mistakes. As I have made clear in previous chapters, it takes practice to "enjoy" learning from one's mistakes. Doing so promptly and openly in the case of your own error very simply helps the leader do a better job on behalf of the organization in the future.

A third lesson, more subtle perhaps, is that the empathy you have shown to your team during their learning process is likely to be returned when you are the one in error and have admitted it directly. Their sensitivity to you is a gift in itself, one whose meaning cannot be overstated. But that display of empathy towards the leader has import for the team as well as for that individual. It improves the team dynamic by offering a kind of "practice" that helps staff members interact with their colleagues.

I discovered these lessons firsthand after eight years in the job of CEO at Beth Israel Deaconess Medical Center, when a mistake I had made garnered a great deal of public attention and caused a high level of stress and discomfort to people working at the hospital. Several people whom I asked to read early versions of this book have urged me not to include this chapter, for fear of opening old wounds. Those wounds were painful for all the first time around. I don't see, though, how I can honestly relate leadership lessons to you and reach the end of this book without including the story. I do so not to justify my decisions leading to the error, but because I think it is important to highlight the leadership lessons derived from this error for others who might benefit from them.

The mistake I made was deciding, shortly after I became CEO, to hire a close personal female friend into a new position where she, first directly and later indirectly, reported to me. She worked at BIDMC for almost eight years. After she had left, a letter of complaint about the relationship was received, and the hospital board reviewed the situation. While giving me a vote of confidence, they concluded that I had made a significant error of judgment in hiring and retaining this employee, and imposed a fine. I agreed with their conclusion: It was a major misjudgment on my part. While there are numerous ramifications of the error, the one most relevant for this book is that I should have realized, but did not, that people in the organization viewed this employee as having special access and privileges because of her friendship with me. Perception of such special treatment inevitably undermines the effectiveness of a leader in building trust and consensus in the organization.

How should a leader handle a difficult situation such as this one? You can't undo your error, but you can try to mitigate the consequences for the people in the organization. My approach on this matter was to advise the staff, in a global email, and to apologize directly. I wrote:

> This will be an uncharacteristically short note from me. Our Board recently received an anonymous letter concerning me and my actions as your CEO. The Board appropriately conducted a review of my tenure here and found an instance in which I exercised poor judgment. I agree that the Board's conclusion is accurate, and I have apologized to them. I now also write to apologize to you for any discredit this brings upon our hospital and the excellent work you do here.

I received dozens of responses to this note, and I was surprised and humbled by the content. Just as I had established an ethic that asked people to forgive one another and learn from mistakes, many people on the staff were willing to apply the same standard to me—even though I had made a clear mistake that could affect them and the well-being of their organization. Here is one example:

> One instance of possibly less-than-perfect judgment simply shows you are human. We walk on, all of us, and learn as we go. Thank you for your kindness in apologizing.

The emails were noteworthy beyond suggesting that people were ready to forgive and move on. It is not that they would forgive and forget. No, they rather drew lessons from my experience to their own jobs.

> Thank you for your characteristic openness and directness. If I am exposed to an imperfection in character or judgment or action I'll only be assured that you, like me, are human. I don't expect a god as my CEO. ... I expect that this too will pass. Then, ever onward to bettering our best.

Now, I know that these letters did not reflect all points of view. There were clearly people who were angry at me or disappointed. Obviously, they would be far less likely to write a note along those lines. As John Maeda found way back in Chapter 3, email is an imperfect medium for communication, especially with regard to highly charged personal matters. Because of this, I felt I had to reach out beyond the email and meet with as many as possible. It was important for people to hear from me in person, and for me to see their reactions face-to-face. So several days later, I met with our 200 supervisors and managers, provided more of the facts of the matter, and repeated the apology. At the end of the meeting, one highly respected person stood up and said something like: "You have honestly explained the situation to us and apologized. That's all we can expect from anyone. We all make mistakes. That's good enough for me." The others in the room nodded and murmured in assent.

But, I was worried whether that was true more generally. For several weeks, many people would avoid looking at me in the hallway, a big contrast from the previous eight years' worth of hearty greetings as I walked through the hospital. What I came to realize, though, is that at least some of them were doing it out of warmth and consideration for me. Although some were angry at me, most were not. It was just that they did not know what to say. Perhaps some felt that they would hurt my feelings if they brought up the issue again. Perhaps others just felt awkward. So, I started to go out of my way to smile and talk with them, to let them know that things had passed and that I was "back in the saddle." While it took a few months, those personal contacts and comfort returned—not for everyone, of course, but for enough people that I could go on and do my job.

Constructing Safeguards
From Your Own Misjudgments

As you read this story, you are probably wondering how I could have been so foolish as to have misjudged the situation that caused all this strife. It turns out that this is a common disease of CEOs and other leaders. When you are engaged in doing your job, and you know you are doing it well, you tend to rationalize away things that should be warning signs— things that you would immediately notice as poor judgment if some other leader were doing them.

Shortly after my misadventures at BIDMC, a highly respected leader of a well-known organization pulled me aside at a conference at which I had set forth this episode in my career. He said, "I have to tell you a story about myself." He had brought on a young female staff member in a mentoring kind of role in his corporation. After several years, my colleague hired a new secretary. Six weeks into the job, she said to him, "Do you know what they are saying about you and this young lady?" He was shocked that anyone could have interpreted what was an entirely appropriate and innocent relationship in the manner in which his whole organization was apparently viewing it.

He said to me, "Isn't there a leadership lesson here? Shouldn't we construct formal mechanisms to keep ourselves from suffering poor judgment or what will be perceived as poor judgment?"

The answer is clearly, "Yes." As we have seen in many situations, it is all too easy to rationalize away things when you are in a position of authority and power. (It is especially easy to do so when you are admired by those in your organization because of what you have accomplished and what you stand for.) But there is little in a leader's background that trains you to be alert to this tendency to rationalize. Generally, you are asked to take on leadership responsibilities because you have done well in previous positions. You are rewarded with promotions because of your substantive judgment, your analytic ability, your strategic insights, your ability to assemble and run a great team. Often, there is nothing in your successful career that has reinforced the need to conduct an accurate assessment of your leadership style or to have real-time feedback about particular actions you have taken.

In my case, after the matter became public, many of my senior management team expressed regret and dismay that they had not taken me aside and pointed out what was going on. It was certainly not the case that they were afraid of me or had no concern for my well-being. It was mainly a matter of not wanting to hurt my feelings!

It turns out, though, that the solution is pretty straightforward. It is based on ensuring that there is a performance review and governance structure that is sufficiently well constructed to protect you from your own errors. The simplest approach would be to require an annual "360 degree" review as part of a leader's term of office. This kind of review would comprise confidential and anonymous interviews of people from various parts of the organization. Those interviews would uncover the leader's "hidden" problems and would enable his or her supervisors to point out concerns and together design plans for remediating them. I don't need to go into all the details of such a review here: They are well documented in the management literature, and many independent consultants are available to carry out this task. The simple point here is that this kind of review should be included in the leader's employment agreement. If it is not requested by the hiring authority, the leader should nonetheless insist on it as a condition of employment—for the good of the organization as well as the person.

Saying Goodbye: Learning About Empathy

Many months later, after all had settled down, it was time for me to move on in my career and leave my CEO job at BIDMC. I sent the staff a final email thanking them for their commitment in making ours a great hospital. Many of the notes I received back were straightforward thank-you notes and expressions of affection. As an indication of how deeply what had happened had affected people, though, some staff members also chose to reflect back on my previously disclosed error and apology.

Remarkably, many people, some with whom I had never dealt, felt that they could communicate with me at a very personal level. I know that some corporate leaders would not care about such a thing—or might even feel it inappropriate. For those people, the job definition is to analyze problems, set forth strategy, and steer the ship, with the crew following orders and being held accountable by their supervisors. They might contend that there should be a distance between the CEO and the staff, that a personal connection is a kind of weakness.

As you can see from this book, though, my approach is based on creating an environment of respect for individual action and accomplishment. I hope I have persuaded you that such a setting is one in which people hold themselves accountable to their own high standards. I have talked about transparency as a tool in helping people do so, but empathy between the leader and the team is the key element of this approach. You cannot achieve empathy without a deep personal connection.

But here is the final lesson from my difficult moments at this hospital, something I had never fully appreciated: The empathy is reciprocal. Indeed, I learned from this chapter of my life that true empathy cannot exist unless it goes in both directions. When you ask people to open themselves up enough to learn, you have to likewise open up yourself enough to learn from them. And just as you would with close family members or friends, you have to let them be part of your healing process when you are in pain.

It is a great gift when staff members feel comfortable enough to offer their help in such a deeply personal way to a leader. I cannot overstate the degree to which this level of personal connection is deeply moving and humbling. I know I will remain ever grateful to those at BIDMC who engaged with me in such a manner.

This book, though, is about coaching and teamwork. I need to move away from what this meant for me. Let's go beyond the personal satisfaction for the leader who is lucky enough to experience the reciprocity of empathy. It is my belief that the display of that empathy from staff members to a leader is an exercise that makes it more likely that they will act in similar fashion with others.

Unlike what I have done in the rest of this book, I cannot provide you with stories to prove this point. While the stories that prove it are occurring every day and in every place in my former hospital, they are not documented. My offer of proof, though, is this final selection from the many good-bye notes I received. As you read it, you have to believe how likely this young nurse and other people were to apply their sentiments well beyond me, to their fellow workers, for years to come:

> I am moved by your letter and want to thank you for all your work. As for any transgressions you may have had, I feel you are only human and we all make mistakes. As I'm sure you know, it is how we handle them that makes us who we are.

CHAPTER 10

"Learning is overcoming your prejudices."

The premise of this book is that you, as leader or coach, have an obligation to support and encourage the personal and professional growth of people in your organization. Yes, you are a steward for the mission of your company or institution, but you must also have a deeply personal commitment to your team. We have talked about the importance of showing respect for the values, commitment, expertise, and ideas of people on your staff. We have talked, too, about the need to be modest about your own role, to take a hands-off approach that allows people to explore and experiment and learn from mistakes.

I have tried to illustrate these themes by telling real-life stories of soccer players and industry professionals. As you have seen, there are a lot of similarities between those goofy teenage girls and the serious professionals in your midst! What do they want? They want to understand their role in the organization. They want to be appreciated. They want to feel the pleasure of a job well done, both individually and as part of a team.[57]

I hope you have enjoyed these stories, but they are more than anecdotes. Underlying them are theoretical bases with generalizable lessons.

Your task as a leader is to take a diverse group of people and help them create a team that will carry out the purposes of your firm or institution. Doing so requires knowledge of how people work together, but most importantly, it requires knowledge of how people learn. Upon what theory of learning can we rely that is most useful in the corporate setting? Here's the one that I have found helpful over the years.

Dr. Rosalind Picard at MIT offers the view that three emotions—interest, distress, and pleasure—form a natural cycle associated with learning.[58] Dr. Picard's theory applies to machine-based learning, where she draws from analogies in

---

[57] In the case of the girls, they also want a really good ice cream or pizza party at the end of the season or after a well-played game! So, too, for your staff. Let's not forget the importance of well-timed food, drink, and social settings.

[58] As described in Sarah H. Wright, "Picard lecture explores computers' affective potential," *Tech Talk*, December 10, 1997, MIT News Office, Cambridge, MA, on the occasion of the publication of Dr. Picard's book, *Affective Computing*, MIT Press, 1997.

electrical engineering and systems control, but it also offers valuable insights for the topic at hand.[59]

The first, most obvious, stage is *interest*. You are curious about the subject and, for whatever reason, are drawn to it. You are excited at the prospect of learning a new skill, new facts, or a new approach to solving some kind of problem.

Perhaps her most interesting phase is the second, *distress*. Those of us who have faced a professor skilled in the Socratic method understand the increased pulse rate and perspiration experienced during the distressful portion of the learning experience. We literally "sweat it out" as our slow-moving minds catch up with the emotional stress of learning a new concept or framework. Likewise, our fellow classmates learn as they watch our distress and feel it along with us. (Perhaps they worry that they will be next called upon, or perhaps they just feel sympathy for us!)

Distress is an appropriate word because learning something requires us to change our framework for looking at an issue, and it is difficult to do that. My calculus professor at MIT, an

---

[59] She notes: "I focus on this particular tri-state cycle because (as an electrical engineer by training) these three states seem like the minimal set needed for building an observable/controllable feedback system, which is another way of describing machines that learn. Interest typifies a 'ready to receive input' state; Distress typifies a 'something went wrong and needs fixing' state; Pleasure typifies a 'something right was done' state. From a simple systems view these are on/off, and pos/neg feedback. While this is an oversimplification, I have found it useful in many aspects of our work." Personal correspondence, February 2005.

esteemed mathematician named Gian Carlo Rota, put it this way: "Learning is overcoming your prejudices." He understood that people are not really good at overcoming their prejudices and in so doing have to work through the discomfort of adopting a new view of the topic.

This is what was going on in the story I told about Peter Brandien back in Chapter 3, when the crew operating the region's electric power grid had experienced a near-miss. The team had done an analysis of the situation and revised their control room training regime but still had not fully adjusted their framework for the kind of problem they encountered. He pointed that out to them.

> "I saw a level of discomfort on their faces because they began to realize that they didn't have complete answers and hadn't designed the retraining to avoid this kind of situation in the future." They went back to work and restructured their protocols.

To borrow an expression from another context, distress is a terrible thing to waste. How you handle it, though, is key. If you handle it by criticizing mightily and assigning blame, you simply excite the flight (or fight!) reflexes of the people you are supervising. When that occurs, learning is, at best, postponed. Remember my story from Chapter 4, when a parent asked me, "Why don't you yell at the girls when they make a mistake?" At worst, you stimulate defensive behavior, often accompanied by a stubborn inability to engage in creative thinking. Instead, you want to use the opportunity presented by the moment of distress to be hard on the problem but gentle on the person.

You are then able to help the person experience the third stage of the learning process, *pleasure*. At this point, the person has perfected the new skill or understanding and is free to enjoy his or her new-found knowledge or capability.

If these are the three stages of learning, they suggest that the most important attribute for the teacher/coach/leader is to be sufficiently empathic with the student/player/worker to understand where he or she is in the learning cycle. Dr. Picard notes that if a mentor has sufficient empathy with the students, she can adapt her behavior when recognizing these stages, resulting in more effective interaction and results. Thus, you can gently apply problem-solving pressure or offer positive reinforcement in a manner consistent with what someone needs to succeed in the new stage of knowledge or skills.

"Oh, this is so simple!"

This is illustrated in a story told by Dhaya Lakshmina-rayanan, a business con-sultant who has taken on stand-up comedy as a second profession. She has a routine about her mother, who immigrated to America years ago.

Dhaya's mom and Dhaya

After a painful transition from a life of poverty in India to a more comfortable life in the United States, her mom decided to go to school. At age 45, she had to take a math proficiency test as part of the entrance process. Her MIT-trained daughter was brought in to help.

Dhaya says, "Let's look at this sample test." Her mom was getting stuck on the transitive property. You remember that one from logic and mathematics: a=b=c, therefore a=c.

Dhaya notes in her routine, "My family was really familiar with transitions, why was this property so hard?" She relates the learning process with her mom:

Mom: "I don't get it, ok, do it again, explain it again."

Dhaya: "OK, if a=b... AND b=c... THEN a=c."

Mom: "You are just saying the same thing you said, again, except slower and louder!"

Then I try to explain it in Tamil, my mother's first language, but I don't know how to say "equals". There is no "A" in Tamil: the various sounds for "A" have 5 characters associated with them.

Dhaya: (speaks the same sentence mostly in English with 1 or 2 Tamil words).

Mom: "So now you are not even speaking in Tamil, you are just saying the same thing, with some unnecessary words thrown in for my benefit."

Dhaya: "Yes, because you weren't paying attention!! I don't know how else to explain this simple thing to you!"

My mother looked at her hands and frowned. She then began to speak in Tamil.

Mom: "In my childhood, no one cared if I had eaten that day. If I was at school, I was out of the way, so it didn't matter to them if I learned anything. That's why I'm not smart like you and your brother."

Dhaya: "Ok, mom, let's take a break. How did you learn English?"

Mom: "TV like *Lucy*, *Carol Burnett*, and *All My Children*."

Dhaya: "Ok, cool, awesome. So what is your favorite show now?"

Mom: "The one with the Jew!"

Dhaya: "Uhhh, can you be more specific?"

Mom: "You know, See N Feld...."

Dhaya: "*Seinfeld*. Oh, OK, now think about Jerry Seinfeld. If Jerry tells Kramer something really important, like a secret (a=b). And Kramer turns around and blabs it to Elaine (b=c), wouldn't that be just like Jerry telling it directly to Elaine (therefore a=c)?"

Mom: "Ohhhh this is simple!"

Dhaya had clearly succeeded in coaching her mom in a manner consistent with what she needed to succeed in achieving the new stage of knowledge or skill development.

After a few miscues, her empathy, perhaps prompted by some old-fashioned motherly guilt, made the learning process easy.[60]

A Short Aside About Neurology

Let me posit that there may be a neurological basis for this description of effective learning. Our brain produces hormones in times of stress, and these chemicals seem to have some role in imprinting key memories in our brain. Our ability to remember vividly President Kennedy's assassination or the events of September 11, 2001 seems to be tied to a spurt of hormonal activity during these traumatic experiences. But scientists have also studied the chemical signals in brains during learning sequences, and they have likewise tied effective learning to the production of these hormones. They find that when information is presented in the context of an emotionally arousing experience, it is much better remembered than if the same material is presented in an emotionally neutral setting.[61]

I do not intend here to delve further into the annals of neuroscience to derive management theories. Rather, I raise the issue to emphasize what good educators know: An element of discomfort in the environment seals in the lessons that need to be learned by an individual. I also posit that the same stages of learning identified by Dr. Picard apply to the

[60] You can hear the actual routine here on Snap Judgment:
http://snapjudgment.org/dhaya-smart-like-you
[61] See, for example, Cahill and McGaugh, "Mechanisms of emotional arousal and lasting declarative memory," *Trends in Neurological Science*, Vol. 21, No. 7, 1998, pp. 294–299.

organization as a whole, in addition to the individuals within the company. The job of the CEO is to have sufficient empathy with the corporate organism to know when to offer positive reinforcement (during the *interest* and *pleasure* stages) and when to positively utilize the naturally occurring discomfort that occurs during the *distress* portion of the learning cycle.

Intentions and Values

It is one thing to consider the mechanisms of the learning process as we discuss the imperative for executive leadership. But we must also consider the context—the nature of the individuals and the teams you face. I assert that the vast majority of people working in an organization are well-intentioned and want to do a good job. Whether they work for a for-profit firm or a non-profit institution, they believe in and want to help carry out the purpose of the organization. They also want to do well for themselves and grow personally and professionally. In short, they want to do well, and they want to do good.

As I have related in many stories here, you can count on people to be driven by an underlying set of values, and part of your job is to reflect those values back to the people you are supervising and help them understand how their values are consistent with those of the organization. In other terms, you want to mine the vein of gold in each person's soul and use it to reinforce the learning process that will allow each of them to excel.

On this question of values, let me pause with one more story, this one from the sewers. One day, while I was head of the MWRA, the regional water and sewer agency, I visited the guys who were working in one of our headworks facilities. A headworks building is where the miles of sewer pipes converge into several large channels and then head in a large underground tunnel to the sewage treatment plant a few miles away. A stage in the transport process is that the wastewater travels through a set of screens, which separate larger solid materials from the liquid flows. Those screens, in turn, are cleaned by mechanical rakes, and the guys working in the facility are responsible for keeping the entire mechanism clean and functional. In short, they literally spend their shift shoveling feces and other sewage-laden material into disposal bins.

During my visit, I asked one of the workers, a high-school educated man who had been on the job for many years, "Why do you work here?" He responded without hesitation, "I am protecting the public health."

And, indeed he was. And I found out, too, that he had a slew of suggestions for how to make the place work better and was deeply interested in programs that we had initiated to give him a chance for personal advancement.

I hope my point is clear. If you can rely on a person in the sewers to have a clear sense of values and purpose, to make suggestions for process improvement, and to respond positively to opportunities for professional advancement, you can find similar attributes among the people with whom you work. That substrate allows you to create effective teams.

Collaboration in a Dynamic Environment

But today's work environment calls for something even more: collaborative creativity among the team. Why? Because the world is changing faster than ever. Staid patterns of relationships among staff—under a hierarchical form of leadership—are unlikely to help a firm design and deliver what it needs to survive and thrive. That is particularly the case for older, apparently stable organizations like hospitals and mature industries, the ones facing the disruption of new technologies, new market relationships, and new pricing regimes. It turns out that soccer *is* a metaphor for what is needed in that respect.

R. Michael Bokena expands on this in an article entitled, "An Alternative Sports Metaphor for Understanding Teamwork as Complex: Soccer."[62]

> I have concluded that soccer is [an] effective metaphor for the pedagogy and practice of teamwork in organizations.
>
> But the important point is that its randomness or chaos is accepted and featured at least as much as the ordered part. Every misstep is not seen as deviation or correctable error; off-target passes are necessary and acceptable risks; missed shots and missed tackles are part of the game. There are very wide parameters for effective play and development, yet few rules for correct play. There are constants, such as "positions"

[62] CBS Moneywatch.com, 2009, http://findarticles.com/p/articles/mi_7525/is_200904/ai_n32334152/?tag=content;col1

or "areas" for which players are responsible (wing, midfielder, forward, sweeper, etc), and there are more or less standardized "runs" or executions that are tactically fundamental; also, certainly there are scripts at certain times (marking for set pieces like free kicks and corners). But the vast majority of the game is played within these very wide parameters. It is complex and creative—in fact once you are about sixteen years old and are assumed to have mastered the technical skills to play the game, most of your development is about creativity—about the multiplicity of choices you can make with what you can do.

Bokena is right on target. Soccer can be seen as a metaphor for creative collaboration in a team. This idea conforms with my argument that coaching soccer can likewise be a metaphor for effective leadership. In this book, we have seen examples of how it can work. I hope you find the lessons drawn here to be useful as you pursue your leadership responsibilities.

Acknowledgements

In September 1989, Barbara Levy greeted me after I came home from work, saying, "I signed up Sarah for first grade soccer today. They needed a coach, so I volunteered you. If you don't want to do it, I will, but I thought you would enjoy it." Well, there was an understatement. Not only did I enjoy it, but it became a passion. So my first acknowledgement goes to Barbara, without whom all the stories in this book and the lessons drawn therefrom would simply have not happened.

My gratitude, secondly, goes to Sarah, who graciously allowed me to be her coach from first grade through the Under-10 game in Dedham (Chapter 5: "Aren't you taking this a bit too seriously?") all the way through that high school team (Chapter 8: "We'll design the warm-up, Coach.").

Over the years, I have been a keen observer of reporters and editors in Boston, and I had a feeling that Jennifer Powell of The Excellent Writers Group would be the right person to help me by editing this book. Beyond her own excellent writing and keen editorial instinct, she has displayed a passion for organizational excellence and accountability. Plus, she has lots of kids, two dogs, and the sense of humor necessary to survive a busy household. She exercised a fine and determined hand in correcting my misstatements, forcing rigor into my generalizations, and otherwise taking an unformed concept into this final product. Where the book fails, it is because I disagreed with her. Where it succeeds, I listened.

Harris Collingwood edited my *Harvard Business Review* article, "The Nut Island Effect," cited here (Chapter 3: "I don't want to be on *that* team!") He returned for a guest stint to help correct disagreements between pronouns and their antecedents, verbs that clashed with their subjects, and conjunctions that didn't seem necessary in the context of the stream of thought in which they appeared. Among other things.

And then that same Sarah Levy, now Persing, returned as a superb copy-editor, finding things that even Harris had left lying on the paper, er, screen.

Early versions of this manuscript benefited immensely from comments by Lisa Zankman, Larry Tye, Warren McFarlan, John Bewick, Bob Ciolek, Jim Conway, Michael Spencer, John Isaacson, Jeff Swartz, Bish Sanyal, Susan Shaw, Bill Taylor, Eugene Lindsey, Peter Brandien, Bob Wachter, Paul Johnson, and John Rowe. Separate from the writing process but highly influential nonetheless, Mary Simmons Motte, Jessica Lipnack, Ellen Lutch Bender, Christopher Barnett, Geri Denterlein, Paula Ivey Henry, Alexandra Drane, Ed Englander, and Peter Bogle offered life lessons and support at critical times. Each person generously reflected an abundance of knowledge and experience in his or her suggestions, and I am grateful. Of course, all errors, omissions, and incomprehensibility are the product of my work, not theirs.

My first mentor in coaching was Dean Conway, who taught me how to teach soccer skills but, more important, by example, taught me how to empathize with players in the learning process. He was followed by Rick Sewall, who explained how to teach fundamental skills, and Gary Beatty, who showed me how to create joyous, well-structured practices.

But all praise and thanks must go to the hundreds of girls I have had the privilege to coach over the years. You have met a few here: Margaret, Tovah, Brooke, Ali. To their parents, too, thanks, for the precious time you have allowed me to have with your children, learning from them every single day on the pitch.

Made in the USA
Lexington, KY
17 June 2013